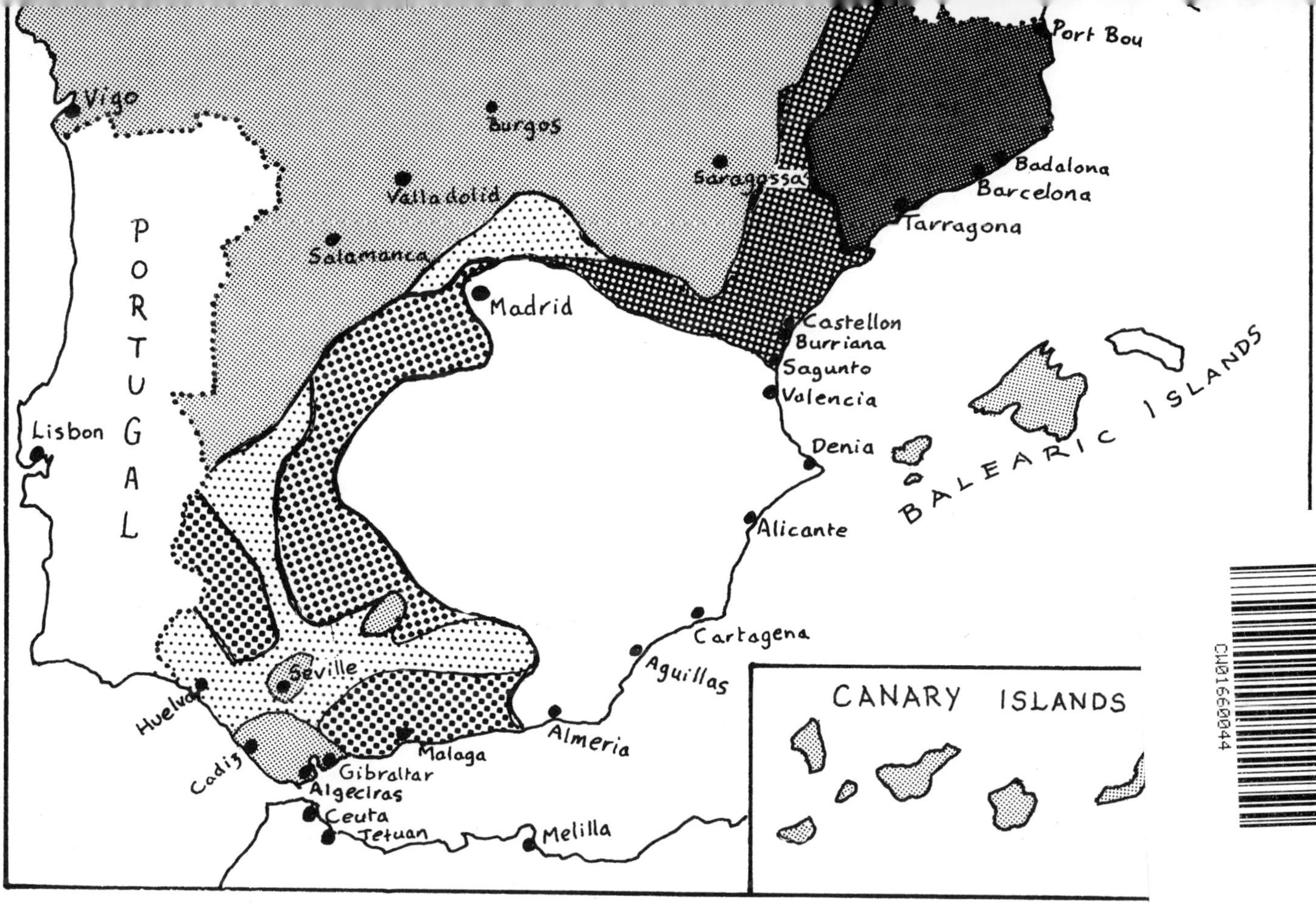
Port Bou
Vigo
Burgos
Saragossa
Badalona
Barcelona
Valladolid
Tarragona
Salamanca
PORTUGAL
Madrid
Castellon
Burriana
Sagunto
Valencia
BALEARIC ISLANDS
Lisbon
Denia
Alicante
Cartagena
Aguillas
Seville
Huelva
Almeria
Malaga
Cadiz
Gibraltar
Algeciras
Ceuta
Tetuan
Melilla
CANARY ISLANDS

WELSH BLOCKADE RUNNERS IN THE SPANISH CIVIL WAR

WELSH BLOCKADE RUNNERS IN THE SPANISH CIVIL WAR

BY

P. M. HEATON

THE STARLING PRESS LTD
PRINTERS & PUBLISHERS
RISCA NEWPORT GWENT
GREAT BRITAIN
1985

ISBN 0 9507714 5 7

Published by P. M. Heaton, Pontypool, Gwent, NP4 0QF

Printed by the Starling Press Ltd., Risca, Newport, Gwent, NP1 6YB

Vivan los Marineros Ingles
Viva la Libertad

Long live English Sailors
Long live Liberty

The People of Bilbao,
April 20, 1937

AUTHOR

Paul Michael Heaton was born at New Inn, Pontypool, in 1944 and was educated at Greenlawn Junior School in New Inn and the Wern Secondary School at Sebastopol. At fifteen he left school and commenced employment, at first in a local store and then with a builders' merchant. A year later he was appointed as a Deck Cadet in the Merchant Navy, with the Lamport and Holt Line of Liverpool, and served in their vessels *Chatham, Constable* and *Romney* usually in the Brazil and River Plate trades. He joined the Monmouthshire Constabulary (now Gwent) in 1963 and has served at Abergavenny, Cwmbran, Newport, the Traffic Department and as the Force Public Relations Officer, and now holds the rank of Inspector.

He has always maintained an interest in maritime history, and since 1977 has had numerous articles published in the magazine *Sea Breezes*. He specialises in the history of South Wales shipping companies, and has had the following books published:

Reardon Smith 1905-1980

The Redbrook: A Deep-Sea Tramp

The Usk Ships

The Abbey Line

Reardon Smith Line

The South American Saint Line

The Baron Glanely of St. Fagans and W. J. Tatem Ltd. (with H.S. Appleyard).

Kaye, Son and Co. Ltd. (with K. O'Donoghue).

ACKNOWLEDGEMENTS

I would like to thank all those who have helped in the compilation of this volume, particularly:—

Mr. F. W. Jones, Cardiff, and his brother the late Mr. H. S. Jones.

Mr. David Burrell, Muirkirk.

Cdr. D. H. Edleston, Fowey.

Mr. R. Wiltshire, Pontypool.

Mr. E. N. Taylor, Gosport.

Mr. Laurence Dunn, Gravesend.

Mr. John Clarkson, Preston.

Mr. A. Duncan, Gravesend.

Mr. K. H. King, Rogerstone.

Mr. F. W. Hawks, Southampton.

Mr. J. J. Wright, Cwmbran.

Mr. K. O'Donoghue, Gravesend.

Mrs. O. A. Roberts, Halstead.

Mr. H. S. Appleyard, Sittingbourne.

Miss M. Urresti, Blackwood.

The World Ship Society Central Record Team.

The National Museum of Wales – Welsh Industrial and Maritime Museum, Cardiff.

Cardiff Central, Newport and Cwmbran Reference Libraries.

World Ship Photo Library.

A. H. Stockwell Ltd., Ilfracombe, for permission to reproduce material from the book *The Scrap Log of an Engineer* by William Patton.

Hugh Thomas, for permission to reproduce material from his book *The Spanish Civil War* (1961).

Mr. C. J. M. Carter, the Editor of "Sea Breezes" for his continued advice.

And lastly to my wife and family for their patience and support throughout.

BIBLIOGRAPHY

Appleyard, H. S. and Heaton, P.M. – The Baron Glanely of St. Fagan's and W. J. Tatem Ltd. (World Ship Society, 1980).

Daily Mail for the period.

Edleston, Cdr. D. H. – Personal recollections.

Echegaray, R. G. – La Marina Mercante y el Trafico Maritimo en la Guerra Civil (Libreria Editorial San Martin).

Francis, H. – Miners Against Fascism (Lawrence and Wishart, 1984).

Gibbs, J. M. – Morels of Cardiff (National Museum of Wales, 1982).

Heaton, P. M. – The Usk Ships (Author, 1982).

Heaton, P. M. – The Abbey Line (Author, 1983).

Heaton, P. M. – The South American Saint Line (Author, 1985).

Jackson, G. – A Concise History of the Spanish Civil War (Thomas and Hudson, 1974).

Jones, F. W. – Personal recollections.

Jones, H. S. – Personal recollections.

Lloyd's List for the period.

Lloyd's Register of Shipping for the period.

Lloyd's Weekly Casualty Reports for the period.

McAlister, A. A. and Gray, L. – H. Hogarth and Sons Ltd – Baron Line (World Ship Society, 1976).

Patton, W. – The Scrap Log of an Engineer (A. H. Stockwell).

Thomas, H. – The Spanish Civil War (Eyre and Spottiswoode, 1961).

Times for the period.

Western Mail for the period.

CONTENTS

LIST OF ILLUSTRATIONS

15. The steamer "Macgregor" which entered Bilbao on April 23, 1937. (*Laurence Dunn*).

16. The "Macgregor" shown under her previous name of "Baron Garioch". (*F. W. Hawks*).

17. Captain Owen "Corn Cob" Jones master of the "Macgregor". (*Western Mail*).

18. Charles Alan Roberts manager of The Guardian Line of Cardiff, which owned the "Macgregor".

19. J. A. Billmeir's "Stanbrook" entered Bilbao on April 23, 1937. (*York Collection*).

20. The Newcastle steamer "Stesso" made it into Bilbao on April 25, 1937. (*York Collection*).

21. The "Backworth" entered Bilbao on April 28, 1937. She had been chartered as a result of public subscription to carry foodstuffs. She is shown under her later name of "Ogmore Castle". (*E. N. Taylor*).

22. Walter Vaughan of Cardiff sold the "Seven Seas Sound" to the Consett Iron Company who renamed her "Leadgate". (*York Collection*).

23. Alfred Pope's steamer "Seabank" evacuated the contents of the Bank of Bilbao and was later seized at La Pallice by the French Authorities. She is seen under her earlier name of "Joyce Llewellyn". (*York Collection*).

24. The "Molten" was captured by the Nationalists off Santander on July 14, 1937. (*Brownell Collection*).

25. Lord Glanely, owner of the steamer "Molton". (*Welsh Industrial & Maritime Museum*).

26. Reginald Jones' "Candleston Castle" (ex "Seven Seas Star") was captured by General Franco's Forces off Gijon on July 17, 1937. (*Welsh Industrial & Maritime Museum*).

27. The Newport registered "St. Quentin" was bombed and damaged by aircraft at Valencia on July 24, 1937. (*York Collection*).

28. The Abbey Line's "Neath Abbey" spent over two years trading to Republican Spain. (*World Ship Photo Library*).

29. Frederick Jones, owner of the Abbey Line, seen as a young man. (*Welsh Industrial & Maritime Museum*).

30. The Barry Shipping Company's "St. Winifred" was bombed and damaged at Alicante during May and June, 1938 with the loss of five lives. (*York Collection*).

31. The "St. Winifred" seen under her earlier name of "Manchester Hero". (*John Clarkson*).

32. The steamer "Isadora" was bombed and sunk at Castellon in June, 1938. She was owned by Stone and Rolfe of Llanelli. (*York Collection*).

33. Claude Angel's "Sunion" was bombed and sunk off Valencia on June 22, 1938. (*York Collection*).

34. The "Dellwyn" was sunk at Gandia on July 27, 1938. She is shown under her earlier name of "Madge Llewellyn". (*York Collection*).

35. Another view of the "Madge Llewellyn" which later became the "Dellwyn". (*Welsh Industrial & Maritime Museum*).

36. The Guardian Line's steamer "Maclaren" was formerly Frederick Jones' "Singleton Abbey". (*Welsh Industrial & Maritime Museum*).

37. Another view of the "Maclaren" of Cardiff. (*York Collection*).

38. Jas. German and Co. Ltd., Cardiff, managed the steamer "Becheville" (seen under her earlier name of "Newton Elm") which was engaged in the Republican trade. (*York Collection*).

39. Claude Angel's "Bramwell", although engaged in the Spanish trade, escaped damage. (*York Collection*).

40. Claude Angel's "Kaolack" was bombed and damaged at Valencia on November 25, 1938.

41. David Barnett's steamer "Cemenco" was also bombed and damaged at Valencia on November 25, 1938. (*John Clarkson*).

42. The steamer "Atlantic Guide" was bombed and damaged at Valencia on February 9, 1939. (*Laurence Dunn*).

43. The Dillwyn Steamship Company's "Bellwyn" refused to submit to a Nationalist warship off Southern Spain on March 10, 1939.

44. The steamer "Transeas" was damaged by bombing in February and March, 1939. She is shown under her earlier name of "Polmela". (*R. M. Parsons*).

45. The steamer "Ronwyn" was engaged in the Spanish trade. She was owned by the Dillwyn Steamship Co. Ltd. (*Laurence Dunn*).

46. The Dillwyn Steamship Company's steamer "Josewyn". (*Welsh Industrial & Maritime Museum*).

47. Stone and Rolfe's "Glynwen" was damaged during the conflict. (*York Collection*).

48. A striking view of the "Philipp M" owned by the Mooringwell Steamship Co. Ltd of Cardiff. (*Laurence Dunn*).

Dust Jacket. Original watercolour by Commander D. H. Edleston, depicting the capture of Lord Glanely's steamer "Molton" by the Nationalist Cruiser "Almirante Cervera" within sight of H.M.S. "Royal Oak". The artist was serving on board the "Royal Oak" and witnessed the incident.

1. INTRODUCTION

Mention the Spanish Civil War to anyone and they will generally think of that conflict in Spain before the Second World War in which the International Brigades fought. Until a few years ago I knew little more about the subject myself. However, having been engaged in compiling histories of a number of South Wales shipowners I noted almost with frustration that the topic kept cropping up in my conversations with those connected with the industry. The name 'Potato' Jones is quoted time and again, and eventually I decided that it was time to find out what the Spanish Civil War was all about, and who this character 'Potato' Jones was.

On July 18, 1936 a rebellion occurred in Spain when the majority of the Armed Forces aided by the Right wing of Spanish politics set about overthrowing the lawfully elected Popular Front or Republican Government which was supported by the Left. Within a month of the outbreak of hostilities half of Spain was in the hands of troops under the control of General Franco. The insurgents or rebels later became known as the Nationalists and were often referred to as the Salamanca or Burgos Government. The Republican Government was often referred to by the right wing British Press as the Reds, but generally were better known as the Republicans, the Madrid Government, and after the move from that beseiged city, as the Valencia Government.

Trade between the United Kingdom and Spain was important to both countries. They needed our coal and we needed their iron ore and pyrites. The iron ore mines around Bilbao were the source of much of the United Kingdom's supplies, and indeed the mines themselves had in decades past been owned by such South Wales firms as the Ebbw Vale Iron Company, the Dowlais Iron Company, Morel and Company and John Cory and Sons. The mineral mines at Heulva were still owned in 1936 by the British 'Rio Tinto' company.

Much of the coal exported to Spain came from the South Wales valleys and was shipped from ports such as Newport, Cardiff, Penarth, Barry and Swansea, and a large proportion of the cargo in each direction was carried in ships owned and/or managed in Wales.

As a result of the war the trade which had hitherto been carried on with a united Spain was now being undertaken with two distinct zones. The insurgents quickly gained control of the sea around Spain and started to exercise a form of influence on foreign (including British) shipping. Apart from an attempted blockade of the insurgent held Cadiz by the Republicans early in the war they had little effect on shipping going to and from ports under the control of General Franco's forces. However, the insurgents from an early stage in the conflict were able to interfere with some of the shipments on route to the Republic.

Ships flying the Spanish Republican flag were being captured and sunk by the insurgent forces. One vessel was even shelled and sunk in the North Sea off Great Yarmouth. The insurgent's interference with these vessels and those flying other flags resulted in an increase in shipments on ships flying the British flag. Non intervention was proposed and after a fashion implemented by the Great Powers, but support for the insurgents was still provided by Germany, Italy and to a lesser extent by Portugal. The Republic was actively supported by Russia and again to a lesser extent by France.

The increase in shipments to the Republicans in British ships resulted in a problem for the British Government, in that whilst privately preferring a Franco style government, they had proposed non intervention. British ships were carrying the vast majority of the cargo and the insurgents controlled the waters around Spain. This meant that it was the insurgents who were stopping the ships, and British ships that they were stopping. The result was to see a higher level of protection being provided outside Spanish Territorial Waters by the Royal Navy than had previously been needed.

Many incidents were reported of British ships being attacked, damaged, captured and sunk, and it is in relation to the activities of the Welsh owned and managed vessels that this book is concerned with, hence the title "Welsh Blockade Runners in the Spanish Civil War". I have started with a review of what the war was about followed by details of the Welsh ships trading to Spain before and during the conflict. Thereafter I have outlined the involvement of Welsh merchant ships throughout each stage of the war.

I hope that you will enjoy reading this book as much as I have enjoyed writing it.

P. M. HEATON
December, 1985

2. THE SPANISH CONFLICT

The Civil War in Spain was primarily a rebellion by the Armed Forces against the lawfully elected Republican Government of the day. Previously, and over countless centuries Spain had been ruled by a Monarchy and subsequent and successive governments had been right wing and based mainly on the Catholic faith. Spain's empire had all but disappeared by the early 1930s, and indeed all that survived was their possessions in North Africa (Morocco) which had cost dearly in effort and Spanish lives to hold, and West Africa.

The elections of 1931 had been a resounding success for the ordinary Spaniard, and a vote of no confidence in the right, the Monarchy and the Armed Forces. Resulting from the election King Alfonso went into voluntary exile, pre-empting what would have been an enforced abdication. In the early years of the new Republic all went well, but by 1934 the murmerings of discontent were to be heard. Although politically left, the Republicans were supported by a wide range of political views largely based on the left, namely by the Anarchists, Socialists and Communists. The ordered life in Spain started to deteriorate from 1934 and was heralded by large scale strikes and disputes, political assassinations, riots and the like.

New elections had been held in February 1936 which for a second term returned a Republican Government, which it was felt by the right was unable to restore order and it was feared was leading the country on the road to Communism. As a result the right wing of Spanish politics based largely on the Fascists, the Catholic Church (although not openly stated), and the landowning classes, with the support and at the instigation of the Army set about plotting the replacement of the Republican Government with one which represented the old values of middle class Spanish life.

The Republican Government realised for some time that all was not well and in anticipation of such a rebellion banished the principal Generals to the outlying areas of the country or empire, where it was hoped that their influence would be less decisive. In this way General Franco had been appointed as the Governor of the Canary Islands and was based at Las Palmas. However the rebellion took place, breaking out on July 18, 1936.

In the early weeks of the conflict the insurgents moved most of the Army of Africa (Moorish troops and the Foreign Legion) to the mainland in Italian and German military transport aircraft. This enabled them to sweep out from the initial centres of rebellion in Seville, Valladolid, Salamanca, Burgos and Saragossa and control the Western half of Spain. The Republican Government was confined to the areas from the Mediterranean coast as far inland as Madrid and the strip along the Northern coast from Gijon to Bilbao.

Although much of the Spanish Navy remained under Government control, the execution of nearly all its officers deprived it of practically all its experienced commanders. Faced with a more modern and numerous insurgent airforce, it spent nearly all the war in harbour and made no attempt to prevent the rebels seizing control of the Straits of Gibraltar.

The Axis powers supplied Franco with ample supplies of aircraft, artillery, tanks and ammunition backed by specialist troops and personnel. The Texaco Oil Company diverted government oil supplies to the insurgents and continued to supply fuel to them on credit throughout the war. The Government were desperately short of all the material of war, especially aircraft, transport and artillery. The Popular Front government in France was eager to meet the Spanish Government's request for supplies but was restrained by hostile criticism at home and by fear of alienating France's only ally, Britain. In Britain, though the Labour and Liberal parties and a majority of public opinion were pro government, the main purpose of the Conservative government was to avoid the conflict starting a general European War and to placate the concern of British financial and mercantile interests, that their considerable holdings were in danger. The poor road and rail links between France and Spain through the Eastern Pyrenees meant that the Republican Government was forced to rely mainly on seaborne supplies. Indeed, when the French later closed the frontier, the sea was the only lifeline. In contrast, supplies for the insurgents flowed freely into the Atlantic ports of Spain and through Portugal where Salazar was strongly pro-Franco.

The Non-Intervention Committee of the major European powers banned the sale of war material to either side, though this was flagrantly ignored by Italy, Germany and Russia. The naval patrols set up to enforce the embargo affected mainly the government side. What seaborne supplies that came to them were subject to attack from the air and "unknown submarines" (known then and proved later to be Italian). Since the insurgents controlled the wheatlands, the Republicans were short of food and in the last year of the Civil War the rations were near starvation level.

The British mercantile marine still affected by the effects of the depression of the early 1930s were eager to capture what trade was available, despite the British Baldwin Government's attempts to deter this. It was this situation which underlies the events recounted in this book.

3. WELSH SHIPS TRADING TO SPAIN

Prior to 1936 a considerable proportion of the cargo carried to and from Spain was consigned in British ships. Spain represented a substantial market for the United Kingdom and in addition to manufactured goods, a large quantity of Welsh steam coal was exported, particularly to the Mediterranean coast ports. Additionally imports from Spain were also considerable. Much of the United Kingdom's supplies of iron ore came from the Bilbao area, minerals from Huelva, and fruit from the Mediterranean ports.

Many of the British ships trading to Spain were owned and/or managed in South Wales. Traditionally vessels of around 4,500 tons deadweight known as the handy sized tramp were engaged in the intermediate trades to and from the United Kingdom, which included Spain. The larger sized vessel of around 7,000 to 8,000 tons deadweight was normally employed on longer voyages such as the River Plate trade, outwards with coal and homewards with grain.

Of the Welsh tramp shipping companies regularly trading with Spanish ports the following were the most prominent. Constants (South Wales) Ltd., formed and managed by the brothers Martin and Halford Constant, had offices at Cardiff and London, and many of their ships although Welsh owned were actually registered at London or elsewhere in the United Kingdom. They owned a large fleet, the majority of which were in the handy sized category, and they had several valuable contracts. Part of their trade was to carry coal out to Southern Spain or West Italy from South Wales and to ballast to Huelva where a cargo of minerals was loaded for the British 'Rio Tinto' company for delivery in the United Kingdom or Continent. Substantial quantities of coal were taken out from South Wales to French Bay of Biscay ports and iron ore then carried from Bilbao to the Bristol Channel on behalf of Guest Keen and Nettlefold Ltd. In addition to shipowning they were also very active in ship broking and many ship sales, particularly in South Wales were handled by them. It is also said that much of the mortgage capital for Jack Billmeir's Stanhope Steamship Co. Ltd was provided by them. Their fleet in 1936 comprised the following vessels.

Name	*Year Built*	*Gross Tons*
Beltinge	1916	1,736
Garlinge	1918	2,012
Gilda Ambatielou	1920	1,138
Hawkinge	1924	2,475
Heminge	1919	2,499
Ightham	1914	1,337
Lottinge	1918	2,468

Name	Year Built	Gross Tons
Lyminge	1913	4,345
Matignon	1922	2,711
Nordeflinge	1913	3,146
Offham	1928	4,062
Ospringe	1910	2,229
Ottinge	1918	1,744
Ruckinge	1923	1,742
Waldinge	1909	2,219
Wrotham	1927	1,884

A firm which tended to employ their ships in the Summer months in the North Russian trade, but was often to be seen loading cargoes of Pyrites at Huelva, usually in the Winter for French ports was Frederick Jones and Company who had offices at 36, West Bute Street, Cardiff. This firm had been founded in 1907 by Frederick Jones who was subsequently joined in the business by his two sons Frederick William and Herbert Stanley Jones, and they managed two shipping companies, namely the Melrose Abbey Shipping Co. Ltd and The Abbey Line Ltd., which had been established in 1911 and 1920 respectively. In 1936 they owned five ships but sold three of them during the Spanish Civil War. However, two new vessels were built to their order during the same period.

Name	Year Built	Gross Tons	Remarks
Singleton Abbey	1915	2,467	Sold in 1936
Tintern Abbey	1924	1,500	Sold in 1936
Margam Abbey	1930	2,384	Sold in 1937
Neath Abbey	1919	2,500	
Melrose Abbey	1936	2,473	
Margam Abbey	1938	2,470	
Tintern Abbey	1938	2,471	Not commissioned until 1939

Frederick Jones and Company's *Singleton Abbey* was actually sold to The Guardian Line Ltd., of Atlantic Buildings, Mount Stuart Square, Cardiff, which had been formed in 1932, and managed since 1935 by Charles Alan Roberts who was in 1940 to become responsible for managing the vessels of Morel Ltd. of Cardiff. This company actually owned three ships in 1936 all of which were acquired in that same year.

Name	Year Built	Gross Tons	Remarks
Macdonald	1912	4,859	Sold in 1937
Macgregor	1919	2,498	
Maclaren	1915	2,330	Formerly the *Singleton Abbey*
Macbrae	1924	2,117	Acquired in 1937

Whilst the *Macdonald* and *Maclaren* were registered at Cardiff, the *Macgregor* and *Macbrae* were registered at Ardrossan and Glasgow respectively. It was not unusual for a Welsh shipowner when acquiring a vessel from other British owners to leave her registered at her previous port thereby saving the cost of registration fees. This small fleet was engaged in the intermediate tramp trades in a similar pattern to Frederick Jones and Company's ships, although the *Macdonald* being a larger vessel, was until her sale, employed in the River Plate trade.

Claude Angel had formed the firm of Angel, Son and Co. Ltd. in 1934 and was operating from offices at Boston Buildings, James Street, Cardiff. He had previously been in business as a shipowner since 1916 trading at first as Claude Angel and Company and later as Angel, Dalling and Co. Ltd. In the early 1930s he had a small fleet, but during the period of the Spanish Civil War expanded to take advantage of the high freight rates on offer. In addition he managed a number of vessels for other owners and was closely associated with Charles Strubin, a Swiss National who was domiciled in London and operated ships under the British and Estonian flags. The Angel fleet comprised the following ships.

Name	Year Built	Year Acquired	Gross Tons	Remarks
Bramhill	1923	1937	1,834	
Hillfern	1920	1937	1,535	
Bramwell	1921	1937	1,927	
Bramden	1925	1937	1,594	
Yorkbrook	1905	1937	1,236	
* *Bellwyn*	1922	1937	1,687	
* *Madge Llewellyn*	1920	1937	1,451	Later renamed *Dellwyn*
* *Marie Llewellyn*	1920	1937	1,464	Later renamed *Kellwyn*
* *Josewyn*	1919	1938	1,926	
* *Ronwyn*	1918	1938	1,766	
Miocene	1911	1938	2,153	
Kaolack	1917	1938	1,837	
Fredavore	1905	1938	1,097	

*These ships were managed on behalf of the Dillwyn Steamship Co. Ltd. which was established early in 1937. At the end of 1938 management was transferred to Stockwood, Rees and Co. Ltd., 20-24, Pembroke Buildings, Cambrian Place, Swansea.

Whilst all these ships were Welsh owned an observer would have been forgiven for not recognising this as they were registered at ports throughout the United Kingdom – Newcastle, Liverpool, London, Swansea, Cardiff and Newport. All were in the 2,000 to 3,000 tons deadweight class and were dry cargo ships with the exception of the *Miocene* which was a tanker.

An interesting fleet was that managed by Walter D. Vaughan through his company – Walter Vaughan (Cardiff) Ltd. from Cory Buildings, Mount Stuart Square, Cardiff. He actually registered the ownership of his ships in various companies, namely the Good Hope Steamship Co. Ltd., the Rising Sun Navigation Co. Ltd., the Anglo-Canadian Shipping Co. Ltd. and the Seven Seas Shipping Co. Ltd., and had prior to 1935 when taken over by Charles Alan Roberts managed the Guardian Line. The 'Seven Seas' ships as they were best known were all registered at Cardiff and were engaged in the full range of the intermediate tramp trades from North Russia to the Mediterranean. However, Walter Vaughan tended to look on ships as assets which were best exchanged for profit, and with the exception of the *Seven Seas Sun* which he kept throughout the period of the Civil War, the remainder quickly changed hands.

Name	*Year Built*	*Gross Tons*	*Remarks*
Seven Seas Sound	1925	2,125	Sold in 1937
Seven Seas Spray	1919	2,579	Sold in 1937
Seven Seas Sun	1924	2,480	
Seven Seas Star	1920	2,494	Sold in 1937
Seven Seas Sound	1919	2,470	Acquired in 1937, sold in 1938

A shrewd character who was renowned for seizing opportunities when they presented themselves was Reginald Jones who traded as Reginald Jones and Co. Ltd. with offices at first at Merthyr House, James Street, Cardiff, but later at Empire House, 51, Mount Stuart Square, Cardiff. He had previously been a partner in McNeil and Jones since 1915 but formed his own company in 1933 to manage the Branch Steamship Co. Ltd. which he had also established in that same year. He never operated a big fleet, and indeed only owned a single ship most of the time. The ship which will be of interest to readers in the following pages is the *Seven Seas Star* which he acquired from Walter Vaughan. He took delivery of the ship at Bordeaux in March, 1937 and subsequently renamed her *Candleston Castle.* Reggie Jones lived at the Brig-y-Don Hotel, Ogmore, Glamorgan, which he owned.

Late in 1936 Alfred J. Pope who lived on the top floor of the majestic Seabank Hotel at Porthcawl, which he owned, decided to enter shipowning to take advantage of the opportunities which were presenting themselves in the Spanish trade. On December 19 of that year he established the Veronica Steamship Co. Ltd., naming the company after his wife, who was the daughter of a well known Porthcawl family, Sir Thomas G. Jones and Lady Jones. Alfred Pope had previously been involved in business at Cardiff as a coal exporter and had sold that business a year or so earlier. He also owned a company called the Kenfig Pool Export and Import Co. Ltd. He was associated in this venture into shipowning with Thomas McEwen who had lived in Spain for thirty years, but was actually described as a merchant trading from an address in Gibraltar. Early in 1937 Alfred Pope acquired the following three ships.

Name	*Year Built*	*Gross Tons*	*Remarks*
Seven Seas Spray	1919	2,579	Late in 1937 renamed *Seabank Spray*
Joyce Llewellyn	1924	1,446	Early in 1937 renamed *Seabank*
Kenfig Pool	1908	2,456	

The two ships *Seven Seas Spray* and *Joyce Llewellyn* which later took names which reflected Alfred Pope's interest in the Seabank Hotel, were both registered at Cardiff in the ownership of the Veronica Steamship Co. Ltd., whilst the *Kenfig Pool* was placed in the ownership of the company bearing that name and having been transferred from the French flag was placed on the British register at Gibraltar. The *Seven Seas Spray* represented another sale by Walter Vaughan. Alfred Pope initially managed the venture from offices at 59, Mount Stuart Square, Cardiff, but later transferred his operations to his hotel at Porthcawl. In addition to the three owned ships he undertook to charter in a considerable amount of tonnage which he time chartered to the Basque and Republican Governments during the Civil War.

During 1936 the Mooringwell Steamship Co. Ltd. was established with offices at Phoenix Buildings, Mount Stuart Square, Cardiff. This company had three directors all of whom contributed to the name of the business, i.e. Messrs Moorsam, King and Howell. Frederick William Moorsam was in business principally as a pitwood importer and the entry into shipowning was merely an extension of this business, in that they now carried their own pitwood to the Bristol Channel from French Bay of Biscay ports. Outwards coal was taken from South Wales to France. Messrs Moorsam and Howell were also in business as garage owners, owning the chain of garages throughout South Wales which traded as Moorwell Motors. This latter business has successfully survived to the present day. In the period up until April, 1939 they owned two ships.

Name	*Year Built*	*Year Acquired*	*Gross Tons*
Jeanne M	1909	1936	1,973
Philipp M	1924	1937	2,085

Specialising in the esparto trade from North Africa to the Firth of Forth was the old established firm of Richard W. Jones and Company of 104, Dock Street, Newport. This firm which was founded in 1875 and entered shipowning five years later was in the hands of a second generation of the Jones family, Guy Treverton Jones and his brother-in-law Geoffrey Ford Rainforth. Outwards from South Wales they normally carried coal to Southern Spain or West Italy. However it is clear that during the entire period of the Spanish Civil War they suspended sailings to Spanish ports. In the period from 1936 their fleet was much reduced from the six ships they had owned in 1929. Their ships were quite outstanding for their unusually smart appearance for a Welsh tramp fleet, and were registered in the ownership of the Uskside Steamship Co. Ltd. and the Uskport Steamship Co. Ltd.

Name	*Year Built*	*Gross Tons*	*Remarks*
Uskbridge	1924	2,466	Sold in 1936
Uskport	1925	2,462	
Uskmouth	1928	2,478	
Uskside	1937	2,706	

A large fleet of ships was operated by Stone and Rolfe Ltd., of New Dock Road, Llanelli and Burrows Chambers, Swansea. The majority of these ships being registered in the ownership of S and R Steamships Ltd. This business had been established by Thomas Stone in 1910 and had changed its title when his brother-in-law had joined him in 1920. They were also associated with the Yugoslav company, Kvarner Brodarsko d.d. In 1936/37 they owned the following ships.

Name	*Year Built*	*Gross Tons*
Goodig	1919	752
Eskwood	1911	791
Glynwen	1923	1,076
Greenawn	1924	784
Hubbastone	1921	873
Isadora	1915	1,212
Monkstone	1923	867
Presto	1916	964
Runnelstone	1923	869
Sarastone	1929	2,473
Lottie R	1937	972

The majority of these ships were coasters which did not normally venture as far South as the Bay of Biscay and beyond. However the Belfast registered *Isadora* and the Llanelli registered *Glynwen* and *Sarastone* were employed in the intermediate tramp trades which included voyages to Spain.

The Ridge Steamship Co. Ltd., of Phoenix Buildings, Mount Stuart Square, Cardiff, owned a single ship which was generally employed carrying coal outwards from South Wales to Mediterranean ports.

Name	*Year Built*	*Gross Tons*
Menin Ridge	1924	2,474

Mordey, Son and Co. Ltd. of 46, Commercial Street, Newport, whose steamer *Gwentland* was sold in 1937 to become Claude Angel's *Bramhill*, replaced her with a newbuilding of smaller dimensions which sometimes reached as far as Northern Spain.

Name	*Year Built*	*Gross Tons*
Gwenthills	1937	868

David P. Barnett of Baltic House, Mount Stuart Square, Cardiff had been involved in shipowning and management since 1916 and by 1936 was managing a single ship, the *Penthames* on behalf of the Golden Cross Line (Bristol Channel) Ltd. However during the period of the Civil War he became responsible for managing a fleet of truly gigantic size which was all registered at London in the ownership of the following companies – the African and Continental Steamship Co. Ltd. (later restyled as the African and Continental Steamship and Trading Co. Ltd.), the Atlantic and Mediterranean Trading Co. Ltd., and the Continental Transit Co. Ltd.

Name	*Year Built*	*Year Acquired*	*Gross Tons*	*Remarks*
Penthames	1909	1936	1,988	Sold in 1937
Penthames	1913	1937	3,995	
African Mariner	1920	1937	6,581	
Sunion	1919	1937	3,110	
African Explorer	1919	1938	4,663	
African Trader	1908	1937	3,825	
Lulca	1907	1938	4,657	
Cemenco	1927	1938	1,887	
Emerald Wings	1920	1938	2,139	
Trade	1912	1938	5,848	
Transeas	1924	1938	1,499	
Transit	1919	1938	3,091	
Atlantic Scout	1912	1938	4,575	
Burrington Combe	1910	1939	4,000	
Atlantic Guide	1924	1939	1,943	

The firm of Jas. German and Co. Ltd., of 68/69, The Exchange, Cardiff had been involved in shipowning since 1919, but in 1936 did not actually own or manage any vessels. In 1937 the Arlon Steamship Co. Ltd. of Greechurch House, 37-45, Greechurch Lane, London, E.C.3, was formed in order to take advantage of the rise in freight rates brought about by the Spanish conflict, and Jas. German and Co. Ltd. were appointed as managers.

Name	*Year Built*	*Year Acquired*	*Gross Tons*	*Remarks*
Arlon	1925	1937	4,903	Tanker
Arletta	1925	1937	4,870	Tanker
Becheville	1924	1937	4,228	

The coal exporters Evans and Reid Ltd., of Empire House, 51, Mount Stuart Square, Cardiff, were responsible then, as they are now, for the export of a large proportion of coal shipments from South Wales to all parts of the world. In 1932 they decided to enter shipowning and management on their own account and to this end established the management business of E.R. Management Ltd. which became responsible for a very large fleet of ships mostly registered at Cardiff, and owned by the following companies – Hector Steamship Co. Ltd., Bantham Steamship Co. Ltd., Nailsea Steamship Co. Ltd., and the Strath Steamship Co. Ltd. The majority of their ships were named with the 'Nailsea' prefix and were of the 6,000 – 7,000 tons deadweight type and were therefore mostly engaged in trades further afield than Spain. But some of their smaller and older ships were regularly to be seen in Spanish ports.

I will mention two other South Wales shipping companies, namely the firm of W.J. Tatem Ltd. which had been founded in 1897 by Lord Glanely, and the B and S Shipping Co. Ltd. which was managing the ships registered in the ownership of the St. Quentin Shipping Co. Ltd., the Triton Steamship Co. Ltd., and the Barry Shipping Co. Ltd. (later to be restyled as the South American Saint Line Ltd.). Both were Cardiff based businesses and operating ships of the larger type which were generally engaged in the River Plate and Canadian trades, but both did use older units of their fleets for occasional voyages to Spain between 1936 and 1939. The ships owned by W.J. Tatem Ltd., although Welsh owned had been registered at London since the 1920s.

I have given details of some of the shipping companies based in South Wales which were engaged in trading to Spain either before or during the Spanish Civil War. These firms were by no means the only ones from the principality engaged in the trade but as readers will see in the subsequent chapters they are those which were the most active and in many cases the most troublesome to General Franco's regime.

During the conflict General Franco often complained that a substantial number of the shipping companies based in the United Kingdom which were engaged in trading to Republican Spain had been formed after the confict began, or if in being prior to July 1936 had expanded their fleets to take advantage of the situation. There was certainly much in what he said.

Of the companies listed above some like Frederick Jones and Company, The Guardian Line, Reginald Jones and Co. Ltd., the Ridge Steamship Co. Ltd., Mordey, Son and Co. Ltd., E.R. Management Ltd., Stone and Rolfe Ltd., W.J. Tatem Ltd., and the B and S Shipping Co. Ltd. were in existence well before the Spanish conflict, and whilst they did trade to the Republic, they were not expanded in order to do so. Generally their fleets of ships were much the same size in 1939 as they had been in 1936. Constants (South Wales) Ltd. was much the same in size also but their ships tended to trade to ports held by the other side in the conflict. Established firms which expanded to take full advantage of the enhanced rates on offer included Angel, Son and Co. Ltd., David P. Barnett and Jas. German and Co. Ltd., whilst the only companies to my knowledge which were specifically set up in Wales to trade to the Republican Government held ports were those under the control of Alfred J. Pope, who nonetheless as will be shown did much to alleviate suffering by sending his ships where others were reluctant to go.

Other companies, like Richard W. Jones and Company ceased trading to Spain altogether during the period, and Walter Vaughan whilst trading to Spain far from expanding actually disposed of ships and contracted his fleet. The Mooringwell Steamship Co. Ltd. although established in 1936 and trading to Spain during the conflict was not set up specifically for the purpose.

4. OUTBREAK OF WAR

With the commencement of the rebellion on July 18, 1936 the insurgents quickly seized control of the Northern part of the country to the North of Madrid, with the exception of the area near to the coast stretching from Gijon in the West to Bilbao in the East. The Balearics (with the exception of Minorca), the Canary Islands, and Spanish Morocco quickly fell to the rebels, but the rebellion at Madrid itself and at Barcelona was successfully put down by troops remaining loyal to the Government. A state of utter confusion reigned throughout the country, and in some areas strikes were called by the government itself in an effort to halt the progress of the insurgents. On the coast, the area on the Atlantic coast to the West of Gibraltar fell to the insurgents within a day or two, giving them the ports of Huelva, Cadiz and Algeciras. Attempts were made to transport troops from Morocco to these ports by sea, but initally the Government were able to command control of the Straits of Gibraltar and many of those attempting to cross were lost or captured. For this reason General Franco, who had flown to Spanish Morocco at the outbreak of the rebellion, made approaches to Hitler and Mussolini, for help, and transport aircraft were quickly placed at his disposal. It was in this way that the Army of Africa arrived in mainland Spain, and in time to ensure the momentum of the conflict was maintained by the insurgents.

The most important port in North Africa to the insurgents was Ceuta which commands a position in North Africa in similar fashion to Gibraltar across the straits. Ships of all nations, both Naval and Merchant were at risk from attack from the outset, as insurgent aircraft set about bombing and machine-gunning shipping in an effort to gain control of the sea. The insurgents appeared to have problems with identification, because a considerable number of neutral ships reported incidents where they had been attacked. Fortunately most of these attacks resulted in no casualties and little damage. Similarly the shore batteries in insurgent hands in North Africa opened fire on just about any vessel which was close enough to the coast to present a target. The Republican forces also made some mistaken attacks on neutral tonnage in the straits, and protests were lodged from a number of nations. Reports were received very early on of shelling of insurgent held territory by Republican naval forces, including Ceuta and Cadiz, whilst the Nationalists shelled the Government held Malaga.

In the North the ports of Vigo and Corunna fell to the insurgents in the early days of the conflict followed by Ferrol and Rivadeo. Two British ships held up at Corunna by strikes at the time of the outbreak of hostilities were the *Ottinge* owned by Constants (South Wales) Ltd. and the Newcastle registered steamer *Hillfern* which subsequently became part of Claude Angel's fleet. The former vessel was undamaged but the *Hillfern* was hit by machine gun fire whilst docked in the inner harbour on July 20. She received damage to her bridge, port holes and her whistle steam pipe, but no casualties were reported amongst her crew. In the South whilst all the activity was going on, no Welsh owned ship was involved in any of the incidents.

During August and September 1936 the insurgents consolidated their positions and had taken control of the entire West of the country. In the North Pasajes and San Sebastian fell to insurgent forces on September 12 and 13 respectively giving them ports to the East of Bilbao.

On June 19, 1936 Frederick Jones and Company had taken delivery of their new steamer *Melrose Abbey* from her builders at West Hartlepool and sent her in ballast to Archangel where she was chartered by a Russian National to carry a cargo of boxboard destined for Las Palmas and Teneriffe. The cargo had shifted on route and on arrival at Las Palmas on Thursday, July 23 she had a 19 degree list to port. Las Palmas was held by the insurgents and as the cargo was consigned to a Russian and the ship had a similar funnel marking to that of the Russian Merchant fleet, she was not allowed to go alongside for the purpose of discharging. However after a period of four days at anchor the problem was sorted out and she proceeded to a berth and commenced to unload, eventually moving round to Teneriffe where completion of discharge was effected. Frederick Jones's son Stanley was on board the vessel at this time, and although the ship arrived only five days after the Civil War had broken out, he remarked how quiet and calm the port was.

The last cargo of pyrites from Spain carried by a ship owned by Frederick Jones and Company before the conflict began was on the *Singleton Abbey* which loaded on May 18, 1936, at which time she was receiving a freight of 9/6 per ton. It was to be November of that year before the next Jones ship loaded at Huelva and the rate had gone up to 11/6 for both of the cargoes carried by the *Margam Abbey*, and the same in January 1937 for a cargo carried by the *Neath Abbey*, all being to either Rouen of Rotterdam. By April 1937 the last cargo taken out of Huelva by Frederick Jones and Company was lifted by the *Melrose Abbey* and was destined for Dublin at the enhanced freight of 12/6 per ton.

No Welsh ship was actually impeded by the insurgent navy in 1936 but a number of ships of Spanish origin carrying cargoes from Welsh ports were intercepted and captured or sunk. The Spanish steamer *Armuru* had a lucky escape. She was intercepted off Corunna on August 26 by an insurgent warship whilst on a voyage from Cardiff to Marseilles with 4,000 tons of coal, and was ordered into an insurgent held port. However, during the night she was able to escape in the darkness, and finally turned up in the safety of Brest harbour.

By September and October 1936 the insurgent navy had asserted control of the Straits of Gibraltar, and was stopping neutral flag ships and in many cases ordering them into Ceuta for inspection. If they were found to be trading with the Republic their cargoes were confiscated, and a number of ships were also seized and subsequently pressed into use by the insurgents. If the ship was found to be on a voyage to a port other than the Republic she was usually quickly released and able to resume her voyage.

Many nations were disturbed by these events, as neither side during the conflict was granted belligerent rights. In time of war it is in order for a nation to stop and search vessels on the high seas. This was not a general war, it was a civil war, and as such the rights of both sides only permitted them to inspect or direct ships which were actually in Spanish territorial waters, i.e. within three miles of the coast. However, the insurgents were to be particularly active in trying to inspect vessels in International Waters. They even declared a six mile limit, but no forces outside Spain would recognise this.

The first incident of real note to affect a Welsh ship on the high seas since the start of the conflict was to involve Claude Angel's Newport registered steamer *Bramhill* on January 12, 1937. The *Bramhill* had left Barcelona on January 6 and after touching Tarragona to complete her cargo she called at Gibraltar for bunkers and was off Cape Tarifa just West of the Straits of Gibraltar when she was approached by the armed rebel trawler *Larache* which fired a shot at her. The *Bramhill* slowed up and immediately sent out a wireless message for assistance. This call was answered by the British cruiser H.M.S. *Sussex* which went to her aid. The *Sussex* requested the rebel trawler to leave, which she did. Thereafter the captain of the *Sussex* caused the papers of the *Bramhill* to be inspected. The ship was carrying a general cargo, and following the inspection she was allowed to proceed on her voyage to Bilbao.

On February 8, 1937 Malaga fell to the insurgents after a bloody battle. The day before, the *Hillfern* which was by now under Claude Angel's ownership, was at this port and due to the heavy bombing of the port by insurgent aircraft the master decided to leave. Shortly after the ship sailed she was intercepted by the insurgent cruisers *Canarias* and *Almirante Cervera* and ordered to stop which she did. The *Hillfern* immediately sent out a distress message which was answered by the destroyer H.M.S. *Brazen*. During this incident the shore batteries at Torremolinos kept firing at the rebel cruisers, but on the intervention of H.M.S. *Brazen* the cruisers left, and the *Hillfern* arrived at Gibraltar the following day escorted by the British destroyer. To further complicate matters the *Hillfern* was found to have two Spanish stowaways on board from Malaga and as a result a guard was put on the gangway of the ship. Subsequently the stowaways were allowed to land and the Welsh owned ship resumed her voyage.

On March 4 the Estonian steamer *Yorkbrook* which was later to form part of Claude Angel's fleet and which he had a hand in controlling at this time was involved in a sea battle off the Northern coast of Spain. The *Yorkbrook* was loaded with 460 tons of war material and had been captured by the insurgent cruiser *Canarias* which was escorting her into the insurgent port of Pasajes. At this time the Republican destroyer *Jose Luis Diez* and four armed trawlers intervened and managed to free the ammunition ship. During the battle a number of the Republican vessels were hit, and one of the armed trawlers was lost with all hands. However, the valuable cargo of arms and ammunition was saved and the *Yorkbrook* brought safely into Bermeo Harbour.

In relation to this action the Basque Government issued a fair amount of propaganda. They alleged that the cargo was on route to the insurgents and they had captured the ship. This was not so, the ship was carrying the cargo on behalf of the Basque Government, had been captured by the insurgents and was recaptured by the Republican forces. According to

R. Gonzalez Echegaray in his book *La Marina Mercante y el Trafico Maritimo en la Guerra Civil* the *Yorkbrook* had delivered arms at Bilbao on three occasions prior to this all in 1936, namely October 10, November 18 and December 3. He also states that the *Hillfern* had delivered arms at Bilbao on November 9 and the *Bramhill* at Alicante on October 1 of the same year. Indeed Lloyd's record the arrival of the *Yorkbrook* in the River Tyne on March 19, from Bilbao, just fifteen days after the action. Conclusive proof that she was working on behalf of the Basque's, as why else would they have let her go.

On March 23 the Cardiff steamer *Menin Ridge* which was carrying a cargo of coal from Barry to Oran was approached in the Straits of Gibraltar by an insurgent armed trawler which ordered her to stop, and fired a shot across the merchant ships bow. Captain Powell of Rumney Hill, Cardiff, master of the *Menin Ridge* refused to comply and maintained his course and speed, and eventually the armed trawler left when a French destroyer appeared on the scene. In a letter home Captain Powell gave the following account.

> While passing through the Straits of Gibraltar I was signalled to by a Spanish Armed Trawler who demanded to know our destination and then he ordered me to stop, or he would open fire. I disregarded both orders and maintained my course and speed. He fired a warning shot, but shortly afterwards a French destroyer came along and the trawler turned back. I reported the matter to the Admiralty at Gibraltar and shortly afterwards H.M.S.*Garland* caught us up and was given particulars of the incident. Our position at the time was 5 miles 330 degrees from Almina Point and outside Territorial Waters.

Resulting out of this incident and two others reported to the Admiralty concerning interference with British merchant ships, the British Naval Commander-in-Chief in the Mediterranean, Admiral Sir A. Dudley Pound sent a protest to the Spanish Nationalist Naval Authorities at Cadiz. The incidents referred to allegations by the insurgents that certain ships were carrying arms to the Republican held ports and the interception of two ships, the Billmeir steamer *Stanholme* and the London vessel *Springwear* with the resulting delays whilst their cargoes were inspected at Gibraltar by the British Naval authorities. In both cases nothing was found.

On March 28 the London registered steamer *Magdalena* which was carrying a cargo of minerals from La Goulette, Tunisia for Bayonne (France) was fired on by an insurgent warship when 20 miles off Santander. The warship fired six shells across the merchant ships bows whereupon she stopped and after being examined by the insurgent was allowed to proceed. The *Magdalena* was owned by the Lensen Company of London and was commanded by Captain James Thompson of St. Michaels Road, Llandaff, Cardiff, who was accompanied on board by his 17 year old son Peter, who was a pupil at Cardiff High School.

Whilst this book is concerned with the Welsh ships trading with Spain I must mention an incident involving the London registered *Thorpehall* which took place on March 30, 1937. This ship was owned by the Westcliffe Steamship Co. Ltd., of London, a company formed on October 23, 1936 specifically to carry cargo for the Republican Government. Of its

Claude Angel's steamer "Hillfern" was the last vessel to leave Malaga before it fell to the Nationalists on February 8, 1937. This ship was involved in a number of incidents during the conflict.

(A. Duncan)

The steamer "Yorkbrook" was captured on three separate occasions by General Franco's forces.
(York Collection)

The "Menin Ridge" refused to submit to a Nationalist Armed Trawler which fired on her in the Straits of Gibraltar on March 23, 1937.

(Welsh Industrial & Maritime Museum)

Captain David John "Potato" Jones, master of the "Marie Llewellyn" who attempted to break the Blockade of Bilbao on the night of April 15/16, 1937.
(Western Mail)

"Potato" Jones photographed at St. Jean de Luz.
(Western Mail)

The steamer "Marie Llewellyn" which was commanded by Captain "Potato" Jones.
(John Clarkson)

The Llanelli steamer "Sarastone" which was commanded by Captain "Ham and Egg" Jones. This ship was directed to Bordeaux for examination by the French Authorities on April 15th, 1937.

(Welsh Industrial & Maritime Museum)

The Sunderland steamer "Brinkburn" left Bilbao with iron ore on April 14, 1937 and avoided capture.
(John Clarkson)

Alfred Pope's "Seven Seas Spray" which broke the Blockade of Bilbao on April 20, 1937. (F. W. Hawks)

The "Seven Seas Spray" shown under her earlier name of "Baron Elibank".

(A. Duncan)

After her capture at Santona and subsequent release, Alfred Pope renamed the "Seven Seas Spray" as the "Seabank Spray".

(Welsh Industrial & Maritime Museum)

Captain W. H. Roberts, master of the "Seven Seas Spray".
(Western Mail)

Alfred Pope, owner of the "Seven Seas Spray".
(Western Mail)

Captain W. H. Roberts and his daughter entertained to a dinner in their honour by Basque Government Ministers following their successful entry into Bilbao.

(Western Mail)

The steamer "Macgregor" which entered Bilbao on April, 23, 1937.
(Laurence Dunn)

The "Macgregor" shown under her previous name of "Baron Garioch".
(F. W. Hawks)

Captain Owen "Corn Cob" Jones master of the "Macgregor".
(Western Mail)

Charles Alan Roberts manager of The Guardian Line of Cardiff, which owned the "Macgregor".

J. A. Billmeir's "Stanbrook" entered Bilbao on April 23, 1937.
(York Collection)

The Newcastle steamer "Stesso" made it into Bilbao on April 25, 1937.

The "Backworth" entered Bilbao on April 28, 1937. She had been chartered as a result of public subscription to carry foodstuffs. She is shown under her later name of "Ogmore Castle".

(E. N. Taylor)

Walter Vaughan of Cardiff sold the "Seven Seas Sound" to the Consett Iron Company who renamed her "Leadgate".
(York Collection)

Alfred Pope's steamer "Seabank" evacuated the contents of the Bank of Bilbao and was later seized at La Pallice by the French Authorities. She is seen under her earlier name of "Joyce Llewellyn",

(York Collection)

The "Molton" was captured by the Nationalists off Santandar on July 14, 1937.
(Brownell Collection)

Lord Glanely, owner of the steamer "Molton".
(Welsh Industrial & Maritime Museum)

Reginald Jones' "Candleston Castle" (ex "Seven Seas Star") was captured by General Franco's Forces off Gijon on July 17, 1937.

(Welsh Industrial & Maritime Museum)

The Newport registered "St. Quentin" was bombed and damaged by aircraft at Valencia on July, 24, 1937.
(York Collection)

The Abbey Line's "Neath Abbey" spent over two years trading to Republican Spain.
(World Ship Photo Library)

Frederick Jones, owner of the Abbey Line, seen as a young man.
(Welsh Industrial & Maritime Museum)

The Barry Shipping Company's "St. Winifred" was bombed and damaged at Alicante during May and June, 1938 with the loss of five lives.

(York Collection)

The "St. Winifred" seen under her earlier name of "Manchester Hero".
(John Clarkson)

The steamer "Isadora" was bombed and sunk at Castellon in June, 1938. She was owned by Stone and Rolfe of Llanelli. (York Collection)

1,000 shares 499 each were held by two Greek Nationals, Messrs Basil Pandelis and John Katepodis, whilst a mere two shares were held by the company secretary Gordon Till who was in fact a British subject. Therefore this was a company, as pointed out by Franco, that was set up to take advantage of the Spanish situation by principally foreign Nationals to get the benefit of British Naval protection.

The *Thorpehall* under the command of Capt. Joseph Andrews was on a voyage from Valencia for Bilbao and had called at Gibraltar for bunkers and having just left this port was signalled to stop by the Nationalist gunboat *Eduardo Dato*. Captain Andrews ignored this instruction and immediately altered course and brought his vessel back to Gibraltar. On the following morning the ship was escorted out of Gibraltar by H.M.S. *Gypsey* and having passed through the straits carried on her voyage alone. But as I will show in the next chapter the Nationalists did not give up.

5. THE BLOCKADE OF BILBAO

The situation in Spain in early 1937 had seen Malaga fall to the Nationalists in the South, but a stalemate existed at Madrid. Franco's troops had reached the gates of Madrid but could get no further, and as a result the Republican slogan 'they shall not pass' was changed to the more appropriate 'they cannot pass'. The successful defence of Madrid had caused the Nationalists to delay their offensive in the North, however, early in April the great push began.

There had been considerable Nationalist Naval activity in the North over the past weeks, and a number of ships had been captured or sunk. The Panamanian flag *Andra* chartered to the Cardiff firm of Emlyn-Jones, Griffin and Co. Ltd. whilst making for Bilbao was on April 5 intercepted by the Nationalist cruiser *Almirante Cervera* in thick fog, shelled and sunk.

Meanwhile the *Thorpehall* with her cargo of food was some eight miles off the Spanish coast on April 6 when she was intercepted by the cruiser *Almirante Cervera* and the armed trawler *Galerna* which fired a shell across her bow. The merchant ship stopped but immediately sent out a distress message which was answered by three British destroyers, the *Brazen, Blanche* and *Beagle.* The British Consul at Bilbao was on board H.M.S. *Blanche* and using a megaphone asked the Nationalists what they thought they were doing. The Spanish persisted in their view that they had captured the *Thorpehall* and as a result the *Blanche* and *Beagle* prepared for action whilst the *Brazen* escorted the merchant ship to the three mile limit off Bilbao. Thereafter the Spanish warships sailed away, showing a disinclination to quarrel with the Royal Navy.

On this same date, April 6, General Franco announced that he would stop all ships from entering ports in Northern Spain, and set about stopping food getting to the Basques. There was already a shortage of food in the Northern territory and news of this blockade came as a considerable blow to the Basques.

The Blockade of Bilbao caused a storm in Britain, where public opinion was firmly on the side of the Republicans and Basques. The political ramifications of the blockade are dealt with at length by Hugh Thomas in his book *The Spanish Civil War* which I can do no better than quote.

> The announcement of this blockade placed the British Government in a difficult position. By international law, a blockade (including the right of search on the high seas) could be carried out by belligerents in war. But specifically because they did not wish to subject British merchantmen to the search of Spanish naval vessels, Baldwin and his Ministers were opposed to the recognition of the two Spanish warring parties as belligerents. Nearly all British trade with Spain was now carried on with Republican ports. But the Nationalists had command of the seas. Therefore, if belligerent rights were granted, it would be mainly Nationalist naval vessels that would be doing the intercepting and mainly British merchantmen which would suffer. But here

was a blockade declared of Northern Spanish ports. Unless belligerent rights were admitted, British merchant ships would be entitled to ask for the aid of the Royal Navy if they were interfered with outside the Basque Territorial waters of three miles from the shore. How much less trouble, therefore, it would be if there were no British merchant ships going to Basque ports at all.

This last reflection, perhaps made only subconsciously, no doubt disposed the British Admiralty to believe certain new reports. The captain of H.M.S. *Blanche* bluntly signalled that the Nationalist blockade was effective. Sir Henry Chilton reported the same from Hendaye. There were other similar naval reports: not only was a Spanish Nationalist naval group outside Bilbao in a position to prevent the entry of all merchantmen; but the Basque territorial waters were mined. Thus (reported Chilton and the Navy) it would be actually dangerous for British merchant ships to try and enter Bilbao. Inside the three-mile limit, of course, the Royal Navy had no right to protect merchantmen. And since the Basques had obviously lost command of the sea, attacks might well be carried out against British ships within the territorial waters. So on April 8 the Admiralty instructed all British merchant vessels within a hundred miles of Bilbao to repair to the French fishing port and resort of St. Jean de Luz, and to await further orders. The following day, Sir Henry Chilton was told by Troncoso, the Nationalist Military Governor of Irun, on instructions from Burgos, that Franco was determined to make the blockade effective. The voyage of four British merchantmen known to be bearing food cargoes and now at St. Jean de Luz would in particular be prevented by force. Meantime, more mines would be laid across Bilbao harbour. This determined statement reached London on the morning of Saturday April 10. It caused Mr Baldwin to summon the Cabinet for Sunday. Back from their week-ends came among others Mr Duff Cooper, Secretary of State for War, Sir Samuel Hoare, the First Lord of the Admiralty, Sir John Simon, the Home Secretary and Mr. Eden, the Foreign Secretary. As a result of the Cabinet, the Board of Trade 'warned' British ships not to go to Bilbao, and intimated that the Navy could not help them if they tried to do so. Mr Baldwin explained this decision to an angry House of Commons on the Monday. There were risks, he said, against which it was impossible to protect British shipping.

Throughout the following week there were mounting uproar in Parliament. All that spring Spain had been an incessant topic for question-time and for debates on foreign affairs. Eden and Cranborne, the Foreign Secretary and his lieutenant, had been hard pressed both by Labour and Liberal sympathisers of the Republic and by the handful of Conservatives who supported the Nationalists. Had the Government heard of the arrival of new Italian divisions at Cadiz? How many Russians were there at Madrid? How many British volunteers had been killed while fighting with the International Brigades? To most of these questions, the Government, concerned above all to maintain and develop non-intervention, had always professed ignorance of exact information. Now the interest of the House of Commons in the cause of Spain reached a climax. On April 14, Mr Attlee for the Labour party moved a vote of censure. The British Government, the greatest maritime power in the world, had given up trying to protect British shipping; yet the Basque President had said that the mines in Bilbao harbour had been cleared, that at night armed trawlers (aided by searchlights) protected the port. Where did the Government gain its information of the dangers? Did it do so from 'those curious people, our consular agents, who seem so silent on the question of Italian troops landing?' Sir John Simon, the Home Secretary, next argued that if British ships were to be allowed to go to Bilbao, there would have to be mine-sweeping. That would constitute intervention in favour of the Republic. Sir Archibald Sinclair, the Liberal leader, argued that the Government's acceptance of the Nationalist blockade spelled intervention. The Germans, after all, he said, recalling incidents of the winter, had always looked after *their* ships. Mr Churchill spoke next. He reiterated his Olympian detachment from either side in the war and indulged in a day-dream of mediation through 'some meeting in what Lord Rosebery once called a "wayside inn" which would give the chance in Spain of peace, of law, of bread and of oblivion'. Then indeed these 'clenched fists might relax into the open hands of generous co-operation'. Mr Harold Nicolson described the refusal to risk British ships in Basque waters as a 'bitter pill. It is not pleasant. It is a potion which is almost nauseating', but it had to be accepted. Mr Duncan Sandys urged the grant of belligerent rights, as only then could one expect the two sides to obey the rules of war. Mr Noel Baker recalled that it was the first time since 1588 that the British had been afraid of the Spanish fleet. Mr Eden ended the debate (which was of course won by the Government) by saying that if British merchant ships did leave St. Jean de Luz, and so disobeyed the Board of Trade warning, they would be given naval protection as far as the three-mile limit. 'Our hope is that they will not go because in view of reports of conditions we do not think it safe for them to go'.

Whilst all this was going on in Britain those British merchant ships within 100 miles of Bilbao were carrying out the instruction given by the Board of Trade. The first ship arrived at St. Jean de Luz on April 8 and by the following day there were four vessels at anchor awaiting orders (and developments). It was here that the legend of 'Potato' Jones was made. Of these four ships three were Welsh owned. The *Marie Llewellyn* managed by Claude Angel of Cardiff and commanded by Captain David John Jones of Waterloo Place, Swansea, was loaded with potatoes destined for Santander, although it has been suggested that this cargo actually concealed arms. Her voyage had commenced at Antwerp. Captain Owen Jones who lived at 16, Victoria Avenue, Canton, Cardiff, commanded the Guardian Line's *Macgregor* which had a general cargo consisting mainly of foodstuffs and grain. The Llanelly registered *Sarastone* with a cargo of foodstuffs, mainly potatoes and grain, from Antwerp, was also commanded by a Captain Jones. The fourth steamer was the Newcastle owned *Hamsterley* loaded with foodstuffs also and commanded by a Captain Still. The fact that three of the masters were named Jones prompted the international press to nickname them, and thereafter they became 'Potato' Jones *(Marie Llewellyn)*, 'Corn Cob' Jones (*Macgregor)* and 'Ham and Egg' Jones *(Sarastone)*.

Interest in the situation at St. Jean de Luz was widespread and was fuelled by the pretended sailings of one or more of the ships, and the statement's of some of the masters particularly 'Potato' Jones who will be remembered in history for his part, deserved or not.

A fifth ship to arrive off Northern Spain since the blockade was declared was the Cardiff steamer *Seven Seas Spray* which was commanded by Captain William H. Roberts, a Cornishman who had previously lived at Penarth, but was now resident at Okehampton, Devon. This ship was on route from Alicante with a general cargo which consisted of drums of olive oil, tinned foods, salt, barrels of wine, cognac, hams, horse fodder and other foods. The master was accompanied by his nineteen year old daughter Florence, and the Chief Engineer's wife Mrs. B. Docker was also on board. When off the Spanish coast she was hailed by H.M.S. *Blanche* who directed her not to attempt to enter Bilbao, her intended destination, but to make for St. Jean de Luz instead. The *Seven Seas Spray* was well outside Spanish territorial waters, and I believe that it was Captain Robert's intention to actually defy the instruction from the Board of Trade which had been reinforced by the British destroyer, and when parallel with Bilbao was going to alter course and enter the port. However, it is plain that the Nationalists also realised this, as the cruiser *Almirante Cervera* met her on April 10 as she made her way along the Basque coast and accompanied her past Bilbao, thus ensuring that she did not enter. The ship arrived at St. Jean de Luz the following day.

On the evening of April 11 the *Macgregor* sailed from St. Jean de Luz and later arrived at Bayonne where she awaited further orders.

Previously the Royal Navy had only kept a small destroyer force on patrol in the Bay of Biscay, but this had been increased to up to four destroyers and was subsequently reinforced by a battleship, H.M.S. *Royal Oak* and a cruiser H.M.S. *Hood* which were based on St. Jean de Luz. Other nations had naval forces off the North Spanish coast including Germany and France.

At this time the Board of Trade reinforced their instructions to shipowners as follows:-

> The Board of Trade desires merchant vessels not to enter Basque ports for the time being on account of the dangerous conditions. We request that instructions be given that vessels should remain at St. Jean de Luz or some other French port, awaiting instructions and co-operating with the Naval Authorities.

On April 12 the Prime Minister, Mr Baldwin made the following statement giving the British Government's attitude in respect of British Shipping trading to ports in the vicinity of the Spanish War zone.

> His Majesty's Government cannot recognise or concede belligerent rights and they cannot tolerate any interference with British Shipping at sea. They are, however, warning British shipping that, in view of conditions at present prevailing in the neighbourhood of Bilbao, they should not, for practical reasons, and in view of the risks against which it is at present impossible to protect them, go into that area so long as these conditions prevail. The Vice-Admiral commanding Battle Cruiser Squadron in H.M.S. *Hood* has been sent to the North Coast of Spain.

On this date the Consett Iron Company's steamer *Leadgate* arrived at Bayonne where she joined the *Macgregor*. The *Leadgate*, although registered at Newcastle, had previously been a unit of Walter Vaughan's fleet and had until a few months earlier been named *Seven Seas Sound*. The ships awaiting orders at this time at St. Jean de Luz were the *Marie Llewellyn, Sarastone, Seven Seas Spray* and *Hamsterley*. At this time Captain 'Potato' Jones started to voice concern about the condition of his cargo of potatoes which he stated was going bad.

Potato Jones publically voiced his opinion of the Nationalist Navy – 'Spanish Navy? Never heard of it since the Armada.' His view of the situation off Northern Spain was similarly flippant 'It makes me sick, thinking of these Spanish Dons strutting about the quarter-decks of their miserable ships intimidating the British Navy and interfering with shipping'. His words endeared him to the British public, and he quickly became regarded as a hero, particularly in his native Swansea. However, the British Government and Royal Navy were less pleased.

At this time the world's attention was focused on St. Jean de Luz, and speculation was rife as to the various masters' intentions. The Royal Navy had instructions to go to the assistance of British merchant ships if summoned, but not to convoy vessels. At this time Captain Still of the *Hamsterley* expressed his willingness to proceed and accompany other vessels, as his vessel was fitted with wireless, while others such as 'Potato' Jones's *Marie Llewellyn* was not. The owner of this ship did not allow him to carry out his offer, or certainly not at that stage.

A spokesman for Stone and Rolfe Ltd of Llanelli, when asked their intention regarding the *Sarastone* said, 'It was on Admiralty advice that she put into port and it will be on their advice that she leaves.' A similar statement was made by the Consett Iron Company regarding their *Leadgate* which was actually in ballast and had been destined to load a cargo of iron ore at Bilbao. On April 14 a spokesman for the Guardian Line dismissed reports that Captain 'Corn Cob' Jones had asked for permission to try to run the blockade, as 'utter nonsense'. But it is interesting to note that on that day the manager Alan Roberts was unavailable for comment as he was in London attending a meeting of the Chamber of Shipping called to discuss the situation.

On Thursday, April 15 after two days steaming outside, due to heavy weather preventing her from docking, the steamer *Magdelena* entered St. Jean de Luz and anchored. It was announced that the Sunderland registered steamer *Brinkburn* had successfully left Bilbao on April 14 with a cargo of iron ore, and in the following days a small number of ships managed to leave Bilbao. However, these ships had been in port prior to the declaration by the Nationalists of the blockade, and it was more the intention of stopping ships entering that they were interested in. This announcement may have influenced some of the masters at St. Jean de Luz and Bayonne, as a number were openly stating that they felt that the effectiveness of the blockade was vastly exaggerated and they doubted that Bilbao was mined.

At 3pm on April 15 the *Sarastone* sailed from St. Jean de Luz having been ordered by the French authorities to proceed to Bordeaux for her cargo to be examined. At 4pm suddenly and without warning the *Marie Llewellyn* weighed anchor and without permission from or informing the harbour master, she set sail from the port. She was observed to be heading on the same course as the *Sarastone* initially, but after an hour or so it was noted from the shore that she was changing course until when she finally disappeared from sight she was facing in the direction of the Spanish coast, and was pitching heavily in the big swell which was running.

Speculation in the world press was aroused by the now famous Captain 'Potato' Jones, who had previously to the blockade been known as 'Swansea' Jones, by the American press was referred to as 'Casey' Jones, and by the Spanish Republicans as Jones 'el Patatero'. *The Times* Correspondent wrote, 'Potato Jones confided his intentions to no one before sailing, but it may be that the honour of being the first to run the blockade will fall to him.' However it was not to be, as darkness fell he was stopped by a British destroyer and turned back, returning to St. Jean de Luz on the following morning. Apparently lurking in the distance ahead of him was a Nationalist vessel which would have intercepted him but for the timely intervention of the Royal Navy. I particularly like the account of this affair given in *The Times*.

> "Potato" Jones, skipper of the *Marie Llewellyn* is an angry man. His attempt to run through General Franco's blockade to a Spanish port – probably Gijon – has failed. After a night spent in battling with a heavy swell the *Marie Llewellyn* crept into here (St. Jean de Luz) this morning a crestfallen ship. Under cover of darkness and dazzling rain, she might have slipped past the Nationalist warships with luck on her side. But the skipper forgot perhaps, that General Franco's warships are not the only watchers on the coast of Spain, and that other high authorities besides those of Salamanca disapprove of blockade running.
>
> It was not a Spanish Cruiser, but a British destroyer that loomed up alongside the *Marie Llewellyn* at midnight and put an end to her wanderings. It was English not in Spanish that "advice" of a kind which could not well be disregarded was winked by flashlight or bawled through a megaphone to her. "Potato" Jones does not admit all this, or, indeed, any of it, to inquisitive journalists.
>
> It is not the least of his sufferings that having failed in his venture, he cannot even divulge in the relief of telling his story. Some mysterious power, emanating by unknown channels from His Majesty's Navy, has struck him dumb. It has done more than that. Not content with silence, it has enlisted his powers of imagination against himself, and "Potato" Jones's powers of imagination are remarkable. The yarn which he spun on his return to harbour combined true ingenuity and apparent bluffness in exquisite proportions. It would be convincing as well as diverting if other sources of truth were not available for its author's undoing.
>
> When I scrambled on board the *Marie Llewellyn* this morning over bulwarks – thoughtfully coated with fresh paint for the convenience of visitors an air of mystery hung over the crew. The seaman who made my boat fast had been pleasantly talkative on Wednesday. Today he would only grin when asked if the voyage had been a success. The mate's description of the night's

escapade was a nod and the words, 'not so bad', murmurred with eyes fixed on the dim Spanish mountains. The intelligent steward, polishing the brass rail on the saloon mantelpiece with a nice blend of domestic devotion and sailorly happiness, remarked brightly that there were too many warships about in these waters. The captain, he added, was having a wash.

On my first visit to the *Marie Llewellyn*, "Potato" Jones, roused from his afternoon nap, had tumbled out of his bunk in his shirt and reached for his trousers with good-humoured tolerance. He now emerged from his bathroom in trousers, only with a light in his eye. Towelling his topsides aggressively, he got his blow in first.

"What do you want?" he demanded – a disabling question – and without waiting for an answer he plunged into the public version of his adventures. "The Spanish coast", he exploded. "Why should I go to the Spanish coast. I can't go there, can I? I can't go against Admiralty orders".

A flash, pure mischief, drove the wrath from his face. "Where the Navy won't go I can't go either, can I; that's fair, isn't it; yes or no? You want to know where I went", he said, "Well, this ship's short of water; I went to Bayonne to get water, and thats' all there is to it. I've got to get fresh water somewhere, haven't I? There's no water-boat here. At St. Jean de Luz I'm offering £5 to anyone who puts it on board; £5 a ton and no takers. 4/- a ton is what I paid at Bayonne. We can't get on without fresh water, can we. So I says to myself yesterday, 'I'm going to Bayonne for water; I'll get into Bayonne by hook or by crook, bar or no bar.' But you know what the weather's been like for two or three days. I tried the bar, and I couldn't get through. Two or three times I tried, but with a big swell running you can't get the bar at Bayonne. Its the most dangerous place in the world to get into. Last time I came out over the bar in rough weather I felt the bottom would drop out of the ship the way she barged down on the water after leaping the swell. You saw me turn West you say? Bayonne does not lie West from here. Did you see me pitching? I had to run head to sea to open water before I could turn."

"Potato" Jones glared fiercely, driving home his words. Livid, but loyal, he swallowed his anger, improving on the silence which had been recommended to him. It seemed unkind to ask awkward questions – why, for instance, should a captain of his experience try to get into Bayonne at night when the place was so dangerous, and everyone knew that the bar was impassable? Followed by the pitying gaze of the steward, we went over the side and ashore together without further reference to the adventures of the *Marie Llewellyn*.

The true story was a little different from Potato Jones's genial romance. It oozed out from various sources during the day. By sailing without notice or permission from St. Jean de Luz and heading boldly for Spain "Potato" Jones had plunged into a complex of forces of which he was blissfully ignorant. To begin with, so long as he was outside Spanish territorial waters he was entitled to protection by the Royal Navy against the very real perils which might beset him. But he had no wireless and his ship was a tiny object for the one British destroyer on patrol to locate. Worst of all, the minefields of Bilbao and Santander – already objects of scepticism to all the British captains – were not, as he imagined, the only dangers in his path. As he ploughed his way Westwards through the gathering darkness his course was leading him straight into the jaws of the battleship *Espana*, which, unknown to him, but well known to the British destroyer, was cruising in his path. By great good luck H.M.S. *Brazen* found the *Marie LLewellyn* and hailed her in time.

Details of the meeting are lacking, but it may safely be supposed that wicked words or their equivalent in electric flashes sped for a time over the deep. Whatever was said "Potato" Jones found the Navy's advice to go home convincing, and added to it a chastened desire to say nothing of his experience.

As for the Navy, it is entitled to consider that it had done its duty by the *Marie Llewellyn* if the rescue of venturesome sailors from the consequences of their temerity may be regarded as a branch of Naval protection.

Back in Cardiff, the ship's manager Claude Angel was giving nothing away. In interviews given to the press he stated that he had no information regarding the *Marie Llewellyn's* attempt to break the blockade, and that if it were true he would have been the first to know. Similarly "Potato" Jones's daughter Mrs. B. Chappell, with whom he lived when at home at Waterloo Place, Swansea, said that when her father was away at sea she rarely heard from him. What she knew of his movements were those she had read in the newspapers. Of her father she said, "He believes in the maxim that if anything happens to him we will hear soon enough." She added, "It is a very anxious time for us, but I suppose he knows what he is about. He is just the sort of man who would do such a thing. He likes adventures and fears nobody". This lady obviously knew her father very well.

Captain David John "Potato" Jones was a well known figure in South Wales shipping circles. He was in fact a part owner of the Dillwyn Steamship Co. Ltd. which owned the ship. Prior to 1924 he had commanded vessels owned by Owen and Watkin Williams and Company of Cardiff. After that he sailed with a number of local shipowners and subsequently retired from the sea. However, after a short period ashore he went back to sea and joined the firm of Claude Angel and Co. Ltd., and had previously commanded their steamer *Bramhill* which had already been involved in an incident with the Nationalist Navy.

However, on Saturday April 17 Potato Jones gave up his attempt to break the Nationalist blockade and set sail for Alicante with his ruined cargo of potatoes. Before he left he answered journalists questions as to his destination with the blunt "Avonmouth". So even after the *Marie Llewellyn* left nobody was sure whether he had really given up the attempt. Historians over the years have actually credited him with breaking the blockage in Northern Spain at that time, but this is definitely not so. The ship arrived at Gibraltar for bunkers on April 23 en route for Alicante where she was to load a cargo of fruit for Antwerp. Meanwhile Claude Angel's steamer *Bramhill* had left Valencia on April 15 on passage for the North coast with a cargo of foodstuffs destined for Bilbao. When asked if this was correct Claude Angel would only say that 'it is far too dangerous for the ship to attempt to enter Bilbao'.

On April 17, in view of the situation off Northern Spain the Chamber of Shipping of the United Kingdom issued advice on the wording of charter parties to be entered into by shipowners contemplating using their ships on voyages to ports affected by the Spanish Civil War. The advice was very comprehensive and is of such interest that I have reproduced it in full.

The Master shall not be required or bound to sign bills of lading for any blockaded port or for any port which the master or owners in his or their discretion consider dangerous or impossible to reach.

If any port of discharge be blockaded, or if, owing to any war hostilities, warlike operations, civil war, civil commotions, revolutions, or the operation of international law; entry to any such port or discharge of cargo intended for any such port be considered by the master or owners in his or their discretion dangerous or prohibited, or

It be considered by the master or owners in his or their discretion dangerous or impossible for the vessel to reach such discharging port

The cargo, or such part of it as may be affected, shall be discharged at any other safe port in the vicinity of the said port of discharge as may be ordered by the charterers.

If no such orders be received from the charterers within 48 hours after they, or their agents, have received from the owners a request for the nomination of a substitute discharging port, the owners shall then be at liberty to discharge the cargo at any safe port which they or the master may in their or his discretion decide on, and such discharge shall be deemed to be due fulfilment of the contract or contracts of affreightment so far as cargo so discharged is concerned.

In the event of cargo being discharged at any such other port the owners shall be entitled to freight as if the discharge had been effected at the port or ports originally designated or to which the vessel may have been ordered pursuant to the terms of the bills of lading.

The vessel shall have liberty to comply with any directions or recommendations as to departure, arrival, routes, ports of call, stoppages, destination, zones, waters, delivery or in any other wise whatsoever given by the Government of the nation under whose flag the vessel sails, or any other Government or local authority, including any *de facto* Government or local authority, or by any person or body acting or purporting to act as or with the authority of any such Government or authority or by any committee or person having, under the terms of the war risks insurance on the vessel, the right to give any such directions or recommendations.

If by reason of or in compliance with any such directions or recommendation the vessel does not proceed to the port or ports originally designated or to which she may have been ordered pursuant to the terms of the bills of lading, the vessel may proceed to any safe port which the master or owners in his or their discretion may decide on and there discharge the cargo.

Such cargo shall be deemed to be due fulfilment of the contract or contracts of affreightment and the owners shall be entitled to freight as if discharge had been effected at the port or ports originally designated or to which the vessel may have been ordered pursuant to the terms of the bills of lading.

The effect of the above being included in charter parties was to ensure payment for the shipowner whatever happened to the cargo or whoever interfered with the passage of the vessel. Payment was due even if the ship was captured and the cargo seized. The trade was not without its risks. The vessels were insured for war risks in addition to their normal policies, and crew insurance was also paid. In addition, after some early disputes with crews, a 50% war bonus over and above their normal wages was paid to the seamen 24 hours before arrival in the Spanish War zone until 24 hours after leaving the zone.

Such was the plight of the people of Northern Spain with near starvation rations, that following the failure of Potato Jones to break through with his cargo, the Basque Government addressed themselves to the masters of the ships awaiting orders and developments at St. Jean de Luz and Bayonne. The offer of special bonuses was made. The sum of 5,000 francs (£50) each was on offer if they left on Saturday April 17, 4,000 francs was offered if they left on the Sunday, and so on, decreasing by 1,000 francs for each day of waiting. The cargoes were urgently needed, and the attention and sympathy of most of the world was focused on the starving people of Bilbao (and other areas of North Spain).

The Basques gave assurances that adequate protection could be given to merchantmen within the three mile limit off Bilbao and that there was no danger from mines as the entrance of the port had been swept. They cited the London steamer *Thorpehall* as an example. This ship had entered Bilbao on April 6 and succeeded in leaving and skirting the coast to enter Gijon in the West on April 19. However the owners of the vessel on realising this, had given orders for Captain Andrews to sail at once for La Pallice (France) and to place himself under the instructions of the Royal Navy, which he complied with. The steamer *Leadgate* which had been at Bayonne had been ordered by her owners to proceed to Brest and subsequently directed that she give up her attempt to enter Bilbao and directed her back to Sunderland.

On April 19 the Welsh steamer *Sarastone* commanded by Captain Ham and Eggs Jones arrived at Bordeaux at the instructions of the French authorities. The non-intervention committee was due to come into force at 12 midnight on that date, and the ship was suspected of carrying war materials. There was considerable support and sympathy in France for the Basque cause and as a result the dockers refused to unload the ship to allow the inspection to be carried out. The dockers had originally consented to unload that part of the cargo which consisted of decaying foodstuffs, but on realising that the Non-Intervention Control Officers were going to take advantage of this to more closely inspect the whole cargo immediately walked off the ship. Whilst the majority of the cargo consisted of foodstuffs, there was a consignment of nickel coins on board which it was feared by the control officers would finish up in the Basque factories to help in the manufacture of munitions. Therefore they declared the coins as war materials. After a week or two the French Trade Union movement allowed the resumption of work by the dockers and after the removal of the offending cargo, and that part of the foodstuffs which had decayed, she was allowed to leave.

At this time, in view of 'Potato' Jones abandoning his attempt to break the blockade, it was felt that none of the other masters at either St. Jean de Luz or Bayonne would be likely to attempt the run. Indeed when asked by a reporter from the *Western Mail* on Sunday April 18, Alfred Pope, the owner of the *Seven Seas Spray* said that it was foolish in his opinion, for any ship to attempt to run the blockade. He had been in contact with London, Paris and St. Jean de Luz and it was not likely that any vessel would try, especially in view of the new Board of Trade instructions. The *Seven Seas Spray* was still at St. Jean de Luz he said, but he expected news regarding her next move within the next 24 hours. Alfred Pope was actually saying what the British Government and General Franco wanted to hear. The Nationalist Naval forces off North Spain were now confident that none of the ships would attempt to break the blockade, particularly in view of the failure of 'Potato' Jones to get through. This view was also held by the Royal Navy. However, Alfred Pope had sent his partner Thomas McEwen to St. Jean de Luz when he heard that the ship had arrived on April 11 to discuss the situation with the master. Alfred Pope had no intentions of giving up the attempt to break into Bilbao, but as a shrewd man he kept his intentions to himself. There was nothing to be gained, but plenty to be lost by declaring his intentions to General Franco's forces.

On the night of Monday April 19 at about 10pm the Cardiff registered steamer *Seven Seas Spray* weighed anchor at St. Jean de Luz and got under way with the intention of attempting to break the blockade. She had not requested permission from the harbour master to leave and had not informed anyone of the intention to go. As those ashore became aware of the departure of the ship they signalled to her to stop, but Captain Roberts ignored them. The ship had no sooner left the port than she sighted a man-of-war which passed her close by. The *Seven Seas Spray* was not displaying any navigation lights, and fortunately the warship did not see her, as it was confirmed that it must have been a Nationalist vessel. As the Welsh merchant ship steamed on her way towards the Spanish coast she was approached by a British destroyer ten miles off the coast which signalled to her, "Where bound?" to which the *Seven Seas Spray* replied "Bilbao". The destroyer warned Captain Roberts that he entered at his own risk, which he accepted, and then wished him good luck. Thereafter the valiant Welsh ship with her valuable and much needed cargo of food continued her voyage towards the Basque port. On arrival in the river she was met by Basque warships and aircraft overhead, and was escorted into the port in triumphant fashion. It was a most moving occasion to those on board the ship, as tens of thousands of inhabitants of Bilbao thronged the river banks to greet them. Captain Roberts and his daughter on the bridge of the ship were almost overcome by this reception and open display of gratitude. Hungry people in the crowds, men women and children, saluted them and shouted, 'Long live the British sailors. Long live Liberty.'

The Basque Government were so grateful for the efforts made by the ship to enter Bilbao that the Ministers of Finance, Commerce and Supply entertained Captain Roberts, his daughter and Thomas McEwen at a dinner in their honour. Captain Roberts was presented with a silver cigarette case embossed with the Basque flag and with an inscription expressing the thanks of the Basque people, while his daughter was given a bracelet.

On hearing of the successful entry of his ship into Bilbao Alfred Pope told newsmen,

> I knew it could be done. My steamer has shown that Franco's blockade is nothing but boast and tommy rot. A British steamer has opened the way for shipping. I hope that the '*Spray* has blazed a trail and shown the rest of the

vessels in St. Jean de luz the way home to Bilbao. She had not the slightest difficulty in carrying her cargo of 4,000 tons of foodstuffs into the port.

She left Alicante some time last week but off Bilbao was told by the Navy that it was dangerous to make for that port. The master, Captain Roberts, made for St. Jean de Luz and communicated with us. Mr. McEwen left immediately for St. Jean de Luz and arrived there on Sunday. He had a talk with the master and members of the crew and thoroughly examined every angle of the situation. Captain Roberts is a Cornishman. McEwen had a talk with him and the crew about the proposition. They were quite agreeable. "Let's go" was their answer to him.

In the meantime I spoke to the insurance people, and they told me that I was not covered if the '*Spray* made for Bilbao. However we agreed to take the risk ourselves, and last night the '*Spray* put out in the darkness for Bilbao. Actually she was only a little way out when an Insurgent warship passed her, but in the darkness could not have recognised her as the ship which was escorted past Bilbao earlier in the week by a rebel cruiser.

I think we have shown up the silly statements made by Franco and his men. Bilbao is wide open, and as long as we get cargoes we shall take them in, whatever the British Navy says or whatever it fails to do for us. A blockade is all tommy rot. After all, we are in business, and considerations for the starving people of the Basque country apart, we had to remember that we had a cargo which might turn rotten on us and be a dead loss.

The Basque Government now tell me that everything is all right and that the way is safe for shipping. My partner and the Captain did the trick themselves. We were determined to get in and we got in. We hope that other people will get in as well. We have been trading to Spain for a long time and never once during this have our ships failed to get where they were chartered for; and if it is humanly possible they never will fail.

Blockade or no blockade General Franco is not going to keep a single one of our ships from going about its lawful occasions. I was certain that what the Basque Government told me was right. I have been dealing with them since the start, and I have never known them tell me anything which was untrue. I have not yet decided on the *Seven Seas Spray's* next port of call. That will depend on circumstances.

Captain Roberts sent his account of the adventure to the *Western Mail* in a long telegram.

Left St. Jean de Luz last night at 10 o'clock after eight days stay. We came out of port and steamed all night without any incidents whatsoever, arriving here at 8am, and receiving an escort of trawlers, battleships, and aeroplanes (in the entry channel only); also covered by shore batteries, which I considered were under the circumstances unnecessary, as no mines or rebel warships were in evidence at daylight. We were challenged by a British destroyer, who asked "Where bound?". Replied "Bilbao". I was informed that I entered at my own risk, which I accepted. Was then wished good luck. The destroyer at St. Jean de Luz had previously said that we would not be able to enter Bilbao and would only have protection whilst outside the three mile limit. (A reference to warning to all merchantment at the French port.) Nevertheless we did it, and it was worth it to receive the great ovation all along both sides of the river from all the people and children. The passage was most normal in every respect. My daughter was not the only lady on board, as Mrs. B. Docker wife of the Chief Engineer, was also on board. I had the loyal co-operation of officers, engineers and crew, and the ladies entered into the venture with zest. I trust this will be the means of other food ships entering the port as I consider there are no risks and cargoes are badly needed.

Roberts, Master – *Seven Seas Spray*.

A proud man who was to be held in very high esteem by the Basques. However, no mention of his attempt to try to persuade his daughter to stay at the French port. Nineteen year old Florence Roberts had in fact written to a friend at home telling of her intention to sail with the ship to Bilbao.

> ... but I am going nevertheless. I am a member of the ship's crew, and although Dad wants me to stay here (St. Jean de Luz) I shall be with the ship when she gets to Bilbao. Make no mistake about that.

How could Captain Roberts have his own way when he had such a determined young daughter.

By coincidence the ship was actually adopted (through the Ship Adoption Society) by Penarth County School for Girls, which Florence Roberts had previously attended. She had written to her former headmistress Miss K. Hughes of her voyage on the ship, giving details of the transfer of ownership of the vessel during the passage, and the details of the cargo which was consigned for delivery at Bilbao. As a result the progress and exploits of the ship were followed by students with great interest and pride.

The arrival of the ship at Bilbao, whilst being welcomed by the hungry people of the city, came as a complete shock to the British Government, the Royal Navy and to General Franco and his Nationalist Navy. The British Government had to admit its mistake in indicating that the port was mined and unsafe, and now gave assurances of protection to ships whilst outside Spanish territorial waters, and instructed the Royal Navy accordingly. The Nationalists were so infuriated by the successful run of the *Seven Seas Spray* that they intensified their blockade of the port, and stated their intention of ensuring that no other ship should make it to Bilbao. The whole world waited with baited breath to see what further developments would take place. Would others follow the *Seven Seas Spray*?

On the day after the successful run into Bilbao by the *Seven Seas Spray*, the Guardian Line's *Macgregor* arrived back at St. Jean de Luz from Bayonne with Captain Owen 'Corn Cob' Jones more determined than ever to make the run. The *Hamsterley* (Captain Still) was still in the port and had already been joined by the steamer *Stanbrook* (Captain Prance). This latter ship was also loaded with foodstuffs (1,840 tons of grain) and was owned by the Stanhope Steamship Co. Ltd of London and managed by that legendary figure of the Spanish Civil War, Jack Albert Billmeir.

On arrival at St. Jean de Luz Captain Jones went on board the cruiser *Hood* which was in port and consulted Vice-Admiral Blake about his intentions. As a result of their discussions it was unofficially agreed that H.M.S. *Hood* would be cruising off Bilbao on April 23, which would be the morning after the *Macgregor* and the other two ships would be leaving St. Jean de Luz.

On the evening of April 22 the three ships, *Macgregor, Hamsterley* and *Stanbrook* left St. Jean de Luz in convoy with their precious cargoes. Nationalist Agents were much more alert by now, and news of their departure was quickly passed to the Nationalist Naval forces, who were determined to stop them at all cost. Unlike the *Seven Seas Spray* these ships had absolutely no chance of taking Franco's forces by surprise. They knew the ships were coming, and realistically the masters of the merchantmen knew they knew. The three British ships expected trouble, and they were not to be disappointed, or at least 'Corn Cob' Jones of the *Macgregor* wasn't, but even he couldn't have forecasted the events which followed.

On the morning of April 23, the ships were by now well spread out. The Nationalist cruiser *Almirante Cervera* accompanied by the armed trawler *Galerna* were patrolling off the coast waiting for them. Fortunately, and to no-one's surprise H.M.S. *Hood* and H.M.S. *Firedrake* were also in attendance. When ten miles off Bilbao the Welsh owned steamer *Macgregor* was fired on by the *Almirante Cervera,* which put a shell across the merchant ships bows. The British cruiser already prepared for action warned the Spanish cruiser not to interfere with British Shipping, and that if she did not cease firing at the *Macgregor* she would be fired upon herself. The *Hood* and *Firedrake* had their guns trained on the insurgent vessels, and fortunately the *Almirante Cervera* stopped firing. At that stage H.M.S. *Hood* told the *Macgregor* to proceed if she so wished. The Nationalists did not give up their attempt to stop the *Macgregor* however. As the Welsh ship was approaching the three mile limit the armed trawler *Galerna* fired another shell across her bows. H.M.S. *Firedrake* quickly intervened and warned the *Galerna* not to interfere with a British ship in international waters. Before any reaction could be forthcoming the Basque shore battery at Bilbao opened fire at the insurgent vessel, which quickly withdrew from range and the Welsh ship which had been fired on twice proceeded towards the port of Bilbao now under the protection of the shore batteries. She entered the port in triumph.

These three cargoes were urgently needed by the Basque people, and again their arrival was watched and cheered by grateful people. Amazingly Captain Prance radioed his owners with 'Arrived 9.30am. Commencing to discharge immediately. Passage from St. Jean uneventful. No sign of mines or Franco. Everything in order and normal.' If his arrival was normal, the ships must have been well spaced out, or were his eyes closed?

Meanwhile other ships were making their way towards Northern Spain. The steamer *Thorpehall* had arrived at La Pallice on April 21 with a cargo of coal loaded at Gijon which she intended to take to Bilbao.

Thereafter the following British ships ran the blockade to arrive in ports in North Spain. On April 25 the Newcastle ship *Stesso* docked with a cargo of foodstuffs accompanied by the West Hartlepool ship *Thurston* also with foodstuffs, both having made the run from the French Bay of Biscay port of La Pallice. On the same date the London vessel *Jenny* with foodstuffs from Antwerp, and the Glasgow registered *Oakgrove* with coal from Sunderland made it into Santander. However, the *Oakgrove* was fired on outside territorial waters by a Nationalist warship, and only made port with the intervention of a unit of the Royal Navy. On the following day the

Sheaf Garth owned by Souter's of Newcastle also made it into Bilbao with a valuable cargo.

On Monday, April 26, 1937 an event was to occur in Northern Spain which was to shock and outrage most of the civilised world. A few miles from the sea lies the small town of Guernica which had a population of about 7,000. This small town, of little military importance to the conflict, was in fact the ancient capital of the Basque Nation. On that date commencing at 4.40pm the German Condor Legions attacked the town and systematically destroyed it in waves of attacks with Heinkel 111 and Junkers 52 aircraft; bombing and machine-gunning the civilian population mercilessly. The centre of the town was destroyed by the end of the attack at 7.45pm, leaving 1,654 people dead and 889 wounded. This single act represented the greatest sin of the war to the Spanish people; it was also the first case in history of the saturation bombing of a defenceless civilian population. Clearly the German and Italian forces were gaining much experience in Spain, and regarded it as a proving ground for their troops and equipment. The world was outraged. General Franco was severely embarrassed, and it was to take over thirty years in Spain before people were publically able to refer to it without fear of prosecution.

The people of Bilbao did not go unscathed either. All through this period Bilbao was suffering heavy air attacks, and indeed General Franco had warned British shipping that they would be specifically sought out as targets. As a result on that day the steamer *Hamsterley*, which had arrived on April 23 was hit and damaged. Fortunately no one was hurt and the damage was not sufficient to stop her leaving the port when she had completed her business.

Attacks had been occurring on neutral tonnage in the Mediterranean on a regular basis. It was clear that whilst some of these incidents were the responsibility of the insurgent forces, it was equally obvious that Italy was behind many of the attacks. Russian ships were being hampered from reaching the Mediterranean ports of the Republic from Odessa in the Black Sea, and ships of many nations were being interfered with. Some ships were being bombed from the air and even torpedoed by submarines, and a number had been sunk. This state of affairs was watched by Britain and France with great concern, and little else at this stage.

At midnight on April 19, actually a matter of hours after the *Seven Seas Spray* had sailed from St. Jean de Luz on her legendary voyage to Bilbao, the Non-Intervention Committee's Naval patrol came into effect. This assigned the Mediterranean part of the Republic coast to Italy and Germany (which seems like a mistake), the Basque/Santander coast to Britain, and the Nationalist held coast to both France and Britain. There was no patrol of the Portuguese coastline, although a few British observers were allowed on Portugal's frontier with Spain and observers were stationed on the French/Spanish border. Non-Intervention Committee control officers were also carried from that date on ships going to and from Spain, thus ensuring as far as possible that arms were not carried.

Very early in the conflict the British Government had banned the export of arms to either side, although, initially this did not prohibit British flag ships from carrying arms, as long as it was from some other country. Later in 1936 they made specific legislation, in the form of the Merchant Shipping (Carriage of Munitions to Spain) Act, 1936, to prohibit entirely the carriage of armaments in British ships. Only one British master mariner was ever charged with the offence, but even he was acquitted. Although a number of Welsh ships were actually suspected by the Royal Navy of carrying arms to Spain, and a careful watch was kept, and examinations made of suspected vessels and cargoes, none was found.

Prior to the breaking of the blockade of Bilbao by the *Seven Seas Spray* on the morning of April 20, the plight of the Basque people was the subject of great concern to many individuals and organisations in Wales, and throughout the United Kingdom. The Trade Union movement were particularly concerned with the well being of the starving people of Bilbao, as was the International League of Friends, and the church. Lloyd George had even publically declared himself to be a 'Basque'. These organisations and people combined their resources and set about attempting to charter a ship to send to Bilbao. Offers of food were accepted and other supplies purchased with donations, and after some difficulty in finding a shipowner prepared to allow his vessel to be used, they succeeded in chartering the steamer *Backworth* owned by the Dalgliesh Steam Shipping Co. Ltd of Newcastle. The ship was loaded at Immingham, and prepared for the voyage. Many people wanted to sail on her, but the owners of the ship insisted that the only people who were to go were those who were needed to sail the ship, i.e. the crew, with the mandatory Non-Intervention Committee Control Officer. At last, on April 23 the *Backworth* set out from Immingham under the command of Captain Russell, on her mission of mercy. She carried a much needed cargo of foodstuffs together with medical supplies and the like.

On April 28, five days after sailing from the United Kingdom, she arrived off the North Spanish coast, and by arrangement was met by the battleship H.M.S. *Royal Oak* and the destroyer H.M.S. *Fury*. At this time the Nationalist warship *Espana* was operating in the vicinity, and at the same time as the *Backworth* arrived declaring her intention to enter Bilbao, the Consett Iron Company's steamer *Consett* arrived off Santander declaring her intention to make that port. The *Espana* actually covered Santander and as a result the *Royal Oak* left the *Backworth* in the charge of the *Fury* and made off to assess the situation further West. Seeing what the situation off Santander was, and that the *Espana* was in attendance the *Royal Oak* warned the master of the *Consett* against trying to make Santander, and in fact the merchant ship altered course to seaward and the following day arrived at St. Jean de Luz.

Meanwhile the *Fury* advised the *Backworth* from trying to enter Bilbao, but Captain Russell, declared his determination to proceed with his cargo to that port at all costs. The destroyer accompanied the vessel towards the three mile limit and then the *Backworth* steamed at full speed towards Bilbao, where she arrived without having been molested by Nationalist Naval forces. Captain Russell on his arrival sent the following radio message to the Press in London via Bordeaux Port Radio, although in parts it was jammed by the Nationalists.

> We nipped in two days ahead in rain swept ocean. Sighted *Fury*, four thirty alongside and megaphoned "You will be bombed or fired on if caught do you intend to proceed Captain Russell". – "We intend to proceed". Cheers from *Fury* and our own crew started (blocked) running three miles (blocked) *Fury* had cleared decks for action. Our enterprise in best tradition of Captain Blood – Backworth had never travelled so fast belching black smoke over bay, took Pilot aboard seven now entering harbour, behaviour of crew magnificent, our lifeboats were all ready expecting fire from Spaniard any minute.

On this occasion the merchant ship was actually assisted by the diversion which was set up by the *Consett* trying to make Santander. The *Backworth* was now the eighth ship to have entered Bilbao since the blockade was broken eight days earlier. The Basques realised that this ship's cargo was rather special as it had been provided by public subscription to help them in their hour of need, and was much appreciated.

The following day four more cargoes were delivered in Bilbao by British ships. At 8am on April 29 the steamers *Marvia* of London, *Thorpehall* of London, *Sheaf Field* of Newcastle and *Portelet* of Guernsey arrived outside territorial waters where by arrangement H.M.S. *Royal Oak* met them. There was no attempt by the Nationalists to prevent their entry, and all four ships made Bilbao without incident. However, not long after their arrival they were attacked by fifteen bombers, which were described by observers as German, which fortunately were unable to score a hit, although damage in the port area was extensive.

A day later the steamer *Consett* again turned up off Santander in an effort to enter the port, but again had to turn to seaward as she was shelled by the *Espana*, which fortunately did not hit her and failed to capture her.

Later that day the British steamer *Knitsley* which was also owned by the Consett Iron Company attempted to make the small port of Castro Urdiales, which is between Bilbao and Santander. On her approach to the coast she was ordered to stop by the Nationalist destroyer *Velasco* which fired a shot, whilst in the distance the battleship *Espana* could be seen. The *Knitsley* had not complied with this order when she heard an explosion from the direction of the *Espana* and then saw a number of Republican aircraft attacking the Nationalist vessel. The reports which were made of this incident were confusing, but whatever, the *Knitsley* saw the battleship sinking and the *Velasco* gave up her attempt to stop the merchant ship to go to the assistance of her countrymen. The *Knitsley* didn't waste any time, and slipped into the port where she took on a much needed cargo of iron ore. Whilst the Republican aircraft had indeed gone to the aid of the *Knitsley* it is apparent that the *Espana* was actually sunk by a mine which she had struck. The loss of this warship by the Nationalists gave the Basque people a much needed boost to their moral.

On this same day the fishing port of Bermeo, near Bilbao, was captured by a contingent of Italian troops, but as the war in the North progressed these soldiers were surrounded and had to beg relief.

Thereafter British merchant ships managed to enter and leave Bilbao with their important cargoes, and were little interfered with. However, the Nationalists increased the effectiveness of the blockade of Santander and Gijon, and as such merchant ships tended to wait in number off these ports, and outside territorial waters for the ideal moment to run the blockade. Some were fired on, and as will be seen in the following chapter a number captured. As regards Bilbao a number of Welsh owned ships were to enter and leave the port, including Alfred Pope's *Joyce Llewellyn* (later renamed *Seabank*), and *Kenfig Pool*, Claude Angel's *Bramhill, Hillfern* and *Yorkbrook*, and Reginald Jones's *Candleston Castle*.

On May 5 the *Hamsterley* was pursued by an insurgent warship as she made her way out of Bilbao to the open sea. Although fired on she succeeded in reaching international waters, and the protection of the *Royal Oak*. It was now becoming apparent that Bilbao was likely to fall to the Nationalists, and as a result many Basque people wanted to leave Spain and escape the consequences of being at the mercy of General Franco's troops. This was reflected in the departure of the *Hamsterley*, as she carried a number of such refugees to safety.

On the evening of that same day and throughout that night 4,000 women and children embarked on the Basque liner *Habana* and motor yacht *Goizeko Izarra* at Bilbao intending to flee to the safety of France. Many were ultimately destined to go on to the United Kingdom where there was considerable support for their cause. However, these two ships left the port on the morning of May 6 flying the Basque flag and that of the International Red Cross. Orders had been given to the Royal Navy by the British Government to protect these vessels from the insurgent threat when, and only when they reached international waters. As a result they steamed at full speed to depart from the three mile limit as fast as possible, where the battleship *Royal Oak* was waiting. Also in attendance and waiting to shell and sink them was the Nationalist cruiser *Almirante Cervera*. These ships, being Spanish could lawfully be interfered with by the Nationalist vessel outside the three mile limit, and the commander of the insurgent vessel plainly conveyed his intentions to the *Royal Oak*, "I have orders to sink the convoy". To which the *Royal Oak* replied, "We have orders to protect the convoy outside the three mile limit". When the refugee ships reached the three mile limit, the Royal Navy set out to protect them by stationing destroyers and the *Royal Oak* around them so that any ship firing at them would also be firing at the British warships. It was an excellent tactic as the Nationalists could not risk this and departed from the scene. These Basque vessels made numerous voyages from Bilbao and later Santander evacuating women and children to French ports, and the *Habana* even took one group of 4,000 to Southampton.

Food shortages in Bilbao were still very apparent. Any British ship delayed in the port also suffered from this problem, and as a result British seamen usually shared out their provisions in these circumstances. A ship leaving port would take with her only sufficient for the passage and leave the balance for their countrymen.

On May 23 the steamer *Oakgrove* was sprayed from stem to stern with pieces of flying metal when a bomb from an insurgent aircraft fell near her. At the time the ship was anchored just inside the harbour at Bilbao. Robert Blackburn, the assistant steward, of Middlesbrough was severely wounded and Joseph Bernadino a seaman of Glasgow was also struck but not badly injured.

In the Mediterranean attacks were still being carried out on merchant ships, and as a result the Republican Government announced that any warship of whatever nationality found to be in Spanish Territorial waters without their knowledge and permission would be attacked by their air force. As a result on the evening of Saturday, May 29 Government aircraft bombed the German battleship *Deutschland* in Ibiza harbour. The ship was not disabled but twenty four German seamen were killed in the attack, 18 seriously injured and 64 slightly hurt. Of the twelve bombs aimed at the vessel four hit their target. The German vessel then proceeded to Gibraltar to land her wounded and dead. In reprisal two days later the German battleship *Admiral von Scheer* and four destroyers shelled the port of Almeria. During this action the shore battery hit and damaged one of the destroyers.

Previously in the war there had been an incident between the Republicans and German Navy. Two German merchantmen were captured and taken into a Basque port where war materials en route to the insurgents were confiscated and a Spanish national arrested. Thereafter the German ships were allowed to leave, but the German Government retaliated by the *Graf Spee* seizing two Spanish vessels in the Bay of Biscay and taking them to a Nationalist held port. Although the crews were released, due to the fact that the Republican's would not release the confiscated cargo and the Spanish passenger, the German Navy handed the two ships over to Franco.

Due to the imminent fall of Bilbao in early June, 1937 thousands of Basque refugees made their way overland to the Santander region trying to escape from Franco's forces. Others managed to leave Bilbao by sea in British merchant ships. Other ships were evacuating Basque refugees from Santander in June. On the 19th due to the extreme shortage of food at Santander five ships embarked refugees for France, these were the Welsh *Hillfern, Kenfig Pool*, and *African Trader* together with the *Surreybrook* and *Latymer.*

June 19 also marked the fall of Bilbao to the Nationalist forces. After an heroic struggle the city fell without resistance on that date as the Basque forces had fallen back to new positions to the West based on Santander. No British ship was left in Bilbao when the city and port fell. One of the last ships to sail was Alfred Pope's steamer *Seabank* (ex *Joyce Llewellyn*) which took with her the contents of the Bank of Bilbao, and other banks including many British. This consisted of securities, records, valuables, money and gold, which the Basque Government were determined should not fall into General Franco's hands. The *Seabank* crossed the Bay of Biscay and cruised around off La Pallice for a week. She then met the Spanish steamer *Axpe Mendi* in French waters and began to transfer her valuable cargo. However, on June 25 both ships were ordered to enter the port of La Pallice and complied when force was used. The two ships which between them had on board 9,000 cases of gold and securities were arrested following an injunction laid by British and Spanish (Republican) banks with branches at Bilbao. Millions of pounds worth of valuables were involved.

The master of the *Seabank* complained to the French authorities through the British Consul at the seizure of his ship, and was informed that it was the cargo which was seized, not his ship, and when it had been unloaded he was free to proceed. Unfortunately, the French dockworkers were very sympathetic to the Basque cause and refused to unload the ship, thus preventing it from leaving. Eventually the French trade union movement allowed the dockers to unload the ship, and her valuable cargo was placed in bond by the French Customs whilst the claims on it were sorted out by the Courts. Thereafter the ship sailed from La Pallice for Santander on August 24.

6. THE BLOCKADE OF NORTHERN SPAIN AFTER THE FALL OF BILBAO

Although historians refer to the blockade of Northern Spain from April to October 1937 collectively as the Blockade of Bilbao, I have for convenience split the period into two chapters; that up until the fall of Bilbao in the preceding chapter, and that after in this.

As a result of the fall of Bilbao, the Basque Government chartered a considerable number of ships to carry refugees from Northern Spain. The ports still in Republican hands, such as Santander, Santona, Musel and Gijon, were crowded with refugees who were trying to flee from the Nationalist advance. This influx of people into these areas caused great strain on the already low food stocks, and the ships entering to embark these refugees in some cases brought food supplies with them. Some ships were actually employed running back and forth between Northern Spain and France only carrying personnel.

A considerable number of these ships were owned or managed in South Wales. Due to the difficulty in separating the various British flag ships, I will mention them all. On June 22 the Hong Kong ship *Marion Moller* was stopped outside territorial waters by the Nationalist armed vessel *Ciudad de Palma*. At this time the *Marion Moller* had just left Santander with as many women and children as she could carry, and immediately sent out a distress call to the Royal Navy. The call was answered by the destroyer H.M.S. *Boadicea* which was sent to her assistance, and on arrival warned the Nationalist vessel, which then left the scene. The British merchant ship was then escorted to St. Jean de Luz where the French authorities refused to allow the refugees to land. Thereafter she was ordered to proceed to Pauillac, near Bordeaux where arrangements were made to handle her human cargo of over 2,000 souls.

On June 30 the Newport steamer *Gwenthills* was approaching the Spanish Coast intending to enter Castro Urdiales to pick up a cargo of iron ore, when she was warned by H.M.S. *Boreas* that the port was now in insurgent hands. She then decided to make for St. Jean de Luz to await orders, but a short while later was fired on by an armed insurgent trawler outside territorial waters. She did not stop and continued for the French port where she arrived the following day.

During July 1937 the Royal Navy were hard pressed to supervise the vast number of British merchant ships which started to lie off Northern Spanish ports awaiting the opportunity to run in to embark refugees. All were steaming outside the three mile limit and also presented a major problem to the Nationalist Navy, who had difficulty in covering all the ports. The British merchantmen knew this and were prepared to wait their best chance of evading capture before proceeding into territorial waters.

On July 4 the French steamer *Tregastel* misjudged her opportunity and was captured by the *Almirante Cervera*. Four shells were fired across her bows before the steamer submitted and was escorted to the Nationalist held Bilbao. The following day, our old friend the *Seven Seas Spray* turned up off Santander with a cargo from Valencia. She was advised by the Royal Navy not to try to enter the port and as a result her master Captain W.H. Roberts made for Bayonne where he communicated with the owner, Alfred Pope, and thereafter awaited orders. The following day the British ship *Gordonia* found it impossible to get past the Nationalist blockade off Santander and made for Bordeaux to await orders. She had actually been stopped by the torpedo boat *No. 7* and the cruiser *Almirante Cervera* before the destroyers H.M.S. *Escapade* and H.M.S. *Bulldog* intervened to rescue her.

The *Royal Oak* was off Northern Spain from July 11 and observed three Welsh owned ships waiting their chance. These were the *Molton* owned by Lord Glanely, *Sarastone* of Stone and Rolfe and the *Kenfig Pool* of Alfred Pope's. The *Kenfig Pool* declared her intention to the British battleship of entering Santander at all costs, but when the Nationalist cruiser *Almirante Cervera* turned up she steamed out to sea again.

Support in Wales for the Basque people was magnificent. A Cardiff Committee of the National Joint Committee for Spanish Relief was established to maintain fifty Basque children at Cambria House, Caerleon, Monmouthshire. The home opened on July 10 and was supported by such influential persons as Lloyd George, Lord Glanely, Professor H.A. Marquand, the Archbishop of Wales and the Lord Mayor of Cardiff.

Lord Glanely, apart from this support in South Wales, had allowed the Basques to charter his two oldest ships, the *Molton* and *Pilton* to carry refugees from Northern Spain. On the morning of July 14 the *Molton* under the command of Captain R.H. Stears, entered the three mile limit off Santander and was captured by the cruiser *Almirante Cervera* within the sight of H.M.S. *Royal Oak* which in view of the merchant ship's position was powerless to intervene.

On July 15 Lieut. Colonel J.J. Llewellyn, Civil Lord of the Admiralty, in reply to a question in the House of Commons concerning the capture of the *Molton* said:

> According to a report which I have recieved from the Rear-Admiral, Second Battle Squadron, who was present in H.M.S. *Royal Oak*, the steamer *Molton* entered Spanish territorial waters opposite Santander at approximately 5.45am yesterday. At this time the Spanish cruiser *Almirante Cervera* was outside territorial waters. When the *Molton* was some distance inside territorial waters the *Almirante Cervera* signalled to her, but these signals could not be distinguished from H.M.S. *Royal Oak*. Subsequently the *Almirante Cervera* fired two warning shots, after the second of which the *Molton* submitted, indicating the fact by altering course and reversing engines. The *Almirante Cervera* ordered the *Molton* to proceed on a Northerly course. Shortly afterwards the *Almirante Cervera* fired another warning shot, whereupon H.M.S. *Royal Oak* intervened and asked why she continued to fire after the ship had submitted. The *Almirante Cervera* replied that she fired because the *Molton* was delaying in carrying out the order. Thereafter the *Molton* steered the course ordered and was taken off under charge of the *Almirante Cervera*. I regret that I am not aware of her present whereabouts. The report I

have received so far does not show that any signals were exchanged between the *Molton* and H.M.S. *Royal Oak* during the incident.

The *Molton* was actually taken to Bilbao, and was escorted there by the armed trawler *Galerna*. A complication at the time of the capture of the *Molton* which took some of the British warships attention was that at the moment that the *Molton* was entering the three mile limit, Jack Billmeir's steamer *Stanhill* decided to leave the port with a full complement of refugees, and successfully made it out into international waters. There was an uproar in the press in Britain, where it was not understood, or they did not want to understand how and why a British man-of-war was powerless to protect a British merchantman whilst in the territorial waters of another Sovereign State. On July 19 Anthony Eden, the Foreign Secretary made the following statement regarding the *Molton*, in the House of Commons:

> I understand that the steamer *Molton* was chartered on July 1 by the Basque Government agent in London for the purpose of evacuating civilian refugees from Northern Spain to French ports. Instructions have been sent to H.M. Ambassador at Hendaye to demand the release of the vessel and of her crew and to state that His Majesty's Government must hold General Franco's Government responsible for any injury or damage she may have incurred. It is reported in the Press that the ship is about to be released. I have not been able to confirm that.

On the afternoon after the capture of the *Molton* the Welsh steamer *Kellwyn* turned up off Santander hoping to enter. This ship was none other than the *Marie Llewellyn* under a new guise, but still commanded by the colourful character 'Potato' Jones. On being warned by H.M.S. *Royal Oak* of the morning's activities she steamed off to the West and entered Gijon which was not so heavily blockaded. This ship brought out 800 refugees.

On July 15 the *Kenfig Pool* put back into Bayonne for bunkers and fresh water, before making further efforts to enter Santander. On that same day two attempts were made by the London registered steamer *Thorpebay* to enter Santander, but on each occasion she was warned against doing so by the two British destroyers lying off the port. The Santander authorities claimed that on both occasions the channel was clear and that no insurgent vessel was in sight.

On the evening of July 15 the Cardiff owned *Nailsea Vale* attempted to enter Santander to take off refugees, but in response to signals from a British destroyer she altered course and steamed away. At the time the cruiser *Almirante Cervera* was in the offing. This merchant ship had previously carried a number of refugees out of this port, and was eventually to succeed again.

The *Sarastone* and Reginald Jones's *Candleston Castle* which had originally intended to enter Santander to board women and children, changed their minds and on July 17 headed for Gijon. Both had been off the coast for some days, and decided their chances would be better further to the West. However as they neared the port of Musel near Gijon and inside territorial waters they were fired on by the Nationalist warships

Valesco and *Plus Ultra*. Unfortunately the *Candleston Castle* was captured and taken into the Nationalist port of Ferrol, whilst the *Sarastone* managed to reach Gijon by sailing close into the coast where she was protected by coastal batteries.

Subsequently Reginald Jones received the following cable from his ship:

> Anchored Ferrol Harbour yesterday, July 18, remaining here pending inquiry, please advise relatives all well on board. British Consul Corunna arrived and rendering us all assistance.

Thus Reginald Jones had lost the use of his only ship for a while. On July 19 the steamer *Jenny* succeeded in entering Gijon while the *Thorpebay* joined the *Marvia* waiting off Santander.

An interesting account of a Welsh owned ship engaged in breaking the blockade at Santander is given in William Patton's book – *The Scrap Log of an Engineer*. This concerned the steamer *Pilton* owned by Lord Glanely:

> The steamer *Pilton*, on which I was serving as Chief Engineer, was about five miles from the port of Santander when a British cruiser detached itself from a number of merchantmen, and made straight for our ship. Her commander hailed us by megaphone:
>
> "What ship?" he enquired.
> "The *Pilton* of London," replied our captain.
> "Where are you bound for?"
> "Santander".
> "What is your cargo?"
> "Coal and salt fish, with two hundred motor cycles."
> "Have you a non-intervention officer on board?"
> "Yes."
> "We strongly advise you not to enter the port."
>
> Our captain decided to explore the situation further. Ahead was a long line of British ships riding on the three mile limit; we steamed up to them, then stopped engines. Between the ships and the shore, Franco's cruiser, the *Almirante Cervera*, moved about waiting for the chance to pounce upon any ship that got within the three mile limit. The distant rumble of gunfire could be heard coming from over the range of mountains where Franco's army, after capturing Bilbao, was pressing on to Santander. Naval advice could not very well be ignored, but we had brought our cargo all the way from England, and our instructions were to deliver it to the Spanish Government forces in Santander.
>
> In face of the uncertainty of the situation, our captain sent a radio message to the owners of the vessel in Cardiff for further instructions. The reply was contradictory: "Proceed to port. Follow advice of Senior Naval Officer." While hesitating what to do next, he received the following message from the Captain of the Port, Santander: "British naval advice is general, and given to all ships. We guarantee protection. The port is quiet."
>
> Our captain hesitated no longer, and he informed the British Naval officer of his intention to attempt to enter port.
>
> "You do so at your own risk," came the reply.

Running the blockade depended upon seizing the opportunity when it arose. The *Almirante Cervera* covered about forty miles of seacoast, guarding the entrances not only of Santander but also those of Gijon and Aviles, and on her patrols she was frequently out of sight, though she had a disconcerting habit of doubling back on her course.

The cruiser could not guard three ports at the same time, however, and the chances of escaping her attentions looked good. At dawn the next day then, with a full head of steam and no sign of the warship, the *Pilton* and two other ships made a successful dash into port. The harbour looked peaceful enough in the bright sunshine and business appeared to be as usual with three British ships working cargo in port. Yet when we got alongside the wharf we soon became aware that we were in a doomed town.

Close by, a mud hopper was reloading a cargo of rotten potatoes that was being discharged on the wharf from the steamer *Backworth*. Such had been the delays encountered that the potatoes had turned bad before they could be put ashore, and now the only thing to do with them was to take them out to sea and dump them. On the quayside starving people spent hours sifting soil from the grain which had fallen in transit from a British steamer to the shore. Children clustered at the foot of the gangplank in the hope that some sailor would throw them a piece of bread or meat. When our steward held out half a loaf of bread the children struggled among themselves to get up the gangplank. But when half way up, they suddenly turned back and ran ashore. A Spanish stevedore hastened off the ship muttering the word, "Peligro".

Then we became aware that sirens were sounding an air raid warning. Soon the Germans were over the town dropping bombs indiscriminately – to them the Spanish Civil War was an appetising hors d'oeuvre before the grand feast of slaughter. These children who roamed the waterfront were orphans of the war. In the confusion of disastrous events, there was no one to take up the task of looking after their welfare, so they formed into packs, hunted about for what food they could get, and at night slept on the beach.

Into the town itself there drifted a never-ending stream of refugees from Bilbao and the surrounding countryside; men, women and children with whatever personal belongings they had been able to save. Dusty, hungry and dog-tired, many of them just flopped down on the pavement, and made their beds there – the schools, churches and public buildings were already full of wounded soldiers and refugees. Thousands of refugees found their way down to the waterfront, sheltering as best they could in railway trucks and open sheds. At night the quayside was lit by innumerable small fires around which destitute families clustered for warmth. It was quite impossible to feed all the people coming into the beseiged town, and as a last desperate resort cargo ships were chartered to evacuate as many as possible to France and England. This was an emergency measure with no time in hand to fit proper accommodation for refugees on ships with a normal complement of thirty-five hands. Carpenters were therefore engaged to fit wooden ladders into the ships' holds, and the refugees were herded down there like so many head of cattle.

The discharge of our cargo took two weeks and every day the distant rumble of gunfire became louder and louder. Air raids became more frequent as the insurgent forces closed in, bombs continued to drop haphazardly in the town. There were no proper air raid shelters. Spies were everywhere, friend and foe mixed not knowing each other. The Government warships in the harbour did not fire on the bombers that came over killing women and children, nor did they go out to try and break the blockade; it was said that the commanders of the two opposing fleets were brothers-in-law. At sea, the blockade was now strangle tight, ships went out, but none came in. Ashore, one had the impression of odd contrasts; of crowded streets and empty shops, of men working feverishly in the town square preparing dug-outs while long queues of women waited outside shops with their ration cards, and over the whole scene the painted ladies smiled wickedly down from balconies, ready to welcome the oncoming conquerors.

How long would Santander hold out? That rested with those in high authority. Already it was whispered that a number of planes were in readiness for their flight. A gripping fear seized the womenfolk that Franco might send in his Moors, as he had done in other towns he had captured, but uppermost in the people's minds was the fear of the bomber. On one occasion thousands of refugees waited all day on the landing-stage to board a British steamer that would have taken them away from all the bloodshed, hunger and cruelty of the civil war. As they were lining up to board the ship the sirens sounded. The refugees became panic-stricken, and a mob cry of fear went up as they rushed away from the ship towards the town, dragging their children after them. The ship could not wait for their return, and hundreds thereby missed their passage to safety. Two British ships, having discharged their cargoes, lay idle at the buoys waiting for the human freight market to rise before helping in the evacuation of the town. The Spanish Government chartered ships at £100 a day, small ships that had been rusting on the scrap heap only a few months ago. But this was not good enough for the shipmongers, and not until the freight rose to £200 a day did they move.

As the fate of Santander became clear, so those in power began to disappear; it was certain death for them to stay. All craft that could possibly do so put to sea with officials and their families on board. In the harbour at night could be heard the muffled noise of slow-heaving anchors from ships attempting to slide out of port under cover of darkness. The skipper of a tugboat came on board to wish me "Goodbye." He had more than once brought his wife and three children on board to shelter in the 'tween decks of our ship during air raids, and it was there I had struck up an acquaintance with him.

"I'm making the attempt tonight," he said.

"Where are you going to?"

"I'll try to make St. Nazaire," he replied. "Others have got there." We learned later that his boat was lost with all hands.

Spaniards who had gone in fear of their lives now openly declared for Franco. The captain and I, going ashore to the agents, were approached in a friendly way by three students. One of them spoke English, and it was plain that his asking for a cigarette was just an excuse to get into conversation with us.

"We three are Falangists," said he. "My brother is fighting in Franco's army. Franco will win. Your Government is our very good friend." We asked him to direct us to the agent's office, whereupon he told us that his father lived in the same block of buildings, and that he would like us to meet him. So we all went to town together, he explaining that his father used to work in Liverpool, but that now he was a prisoner. His father turned out to be a middle-aged man with more than a clerical stoop, and while he was eager to talk to us he was evidently very nervous at our visit. When he spoke it was in a whisper, his eyes darting here and there while telling us that he was confined to his room, and that he expected to be shot for reprisals against air raids. He must have dreaded to hear every knock at his door. His one need from us was a bunch of old English newspapers. These we were later able to supply him with, along with a few packets of cigarettes and a half pound of tea.

An elderly English lady came on board for lunch one day. She was very outspoken. "I know what I would do with this mob here. Shoot the lot. I've told them so. I've told them the sooner Franco comes and takes over the better."

She told us of the fate of the lighthouse keeper of Santander. It appears that the King's palace, on top of the hill overlooking the harbour, was used as a prison during the early part of the war, and that as reprisals prisoners were dispatched over the cliffs from time to time. The lighthouse keeper asked to be relieved of his post; he said he could not bear to hear the shrieks of women as they were hurled over the cliffs into the sea below. His plea was ignored and three nights later the lights went out. An investigating party found that the lighthouse keeper had committed suicide.

Students paraded the streets during the day, Franco's Fifth Column, and at night revolver fights became increasingly common on the waterfront. Looting started as fewer uniforms were seen. It was then that a party was formed, and flying the white flag, went out to meet the insurgent general. The fighting spirit of the people had been crushed out of them – the bomber had seen to that. It was the grim scene once more re-enacted in which the cry of the people was murderously throttled.

Just before Santander fell to Franco, the *Pilton* took on board 2,500 refugees. It was a silent procession that filed up the gangplank, old men and women, sad-faced children clasping their dolls and toy planes, and girls whose faces lit up when they stepped on the deck, glad enough no doubt to escape from the horrors of the Civil War. No men of military age were allowed to come on the ship. Relatives and friends of the refugees who had come to see them off were barricaded behind hastily erected fences on the quayside. Now and again a man would break through the barricade for a last embrace of his wife and children. For the rest, the men stood silently by, watching their womenfolk board the ship. We were to take the refugees across the Bay of Biscay to St. Nazaire. Out to sea, beyond the three mile limit, was the outline of a number of British merchantmen, while manoeuvring off the port was the *Almirante Cervera*. Further away, British warships watched for developments. We were not interfered with on our way out into the open, but the refugees were plainly alarmed at the sight of Franco's warship, and the name of *'Cervera* was on everyone's lips.

But they soon had something else to worry about when we got over the bar and plunged into the heavy ground swell, for then the ship began to roll causing the utmost confusion among the people as they staggered about in all directions. The bulwarks were lined with women and children vomiting and retching over the ship's side. The decks became slippery, and what with people falling down and babies crying, and groans coming up from the depths of the holds, it was truly a most remarkable state of affairs. The Spanish doctors and nurses who were travelling with us had to start on their job at once.

As night approached the refugees, exhausted by the trials of the day, lay down in utter despair. Most of them were stowed in the holds, where they made their beds with their bundles as best they could on the iron tank tops. Looking down from the hatchway, in the glare of the electric light, they seemed like a swarm of crawling insects. A group of girls took up their quarters on the boat deck; some even ventured into the lifeboats, where they were not exposed to the weather. A dozen women were allowed to put up in the saloon, sleeping on the settees and on the floor, others crowded the forecastle and cabins.

Having seen the change of watches at midnight in the engine room, and satisfied that everything was running well, I retired to my room. Shortly afterwards a knock came to my door, and without hesitation one of the nurses stepped in. I recognised her as the one that I had taken on a tour of inspection earlier in the day to familiarize her with the various departments of the ship.

She said to me, "Tonight I am your wife."

I already had three Spanish women sleeping in my cabin, one on the settee and two on the floor; I had intended to reserve the bunk for myself, but the nurse had other ideas born of desperation. She looked round my room and her eyes fixed on my bookcase. She drew some papers from inside her blouse and placed them between the leaves of one of the books. Then she took off her shoes and got into my bunk.

"The *'Cervera* is following us," she explained. "They will take me away."

"Nonsense," I said. "They would not dare to attack us, we're outside the three mile limit." This in no way reassured the girl.

"They will shoot me," she said, as if to herself.

Putting two and two together I concluded that she was a Communist. She told the other women in my cabin that the *'Cervera* was near, and the ensuing wailing drove me on deck. Here there was more wailing, for the other nurses, five of them, were bordering on hysterics; one was beating her forehead with her fists and beseeching the aid of the saints, while another lay on the bunker hatch moaning and shuddering.

To one more composed than the rest I asked what they were afraid of, and she pointed out to sea and said, "The *'Cervera* is coming to take all of us girls." I looked out to sea and could discern the massive sides of a ship converging on us; not a light was showing on her and the stillness of night was undisturbed by her approach she certainly looked a sinister object. Just then, however, our ship was lit up by a flash of light which dazzled the eyes and, if possible, increased the terror among the nurses. But in reality it was a searchlight from one of our own cruisers. This I explained to the girls, and it had a calming effect on them. The cruiser thrust herself between the two ships, raking the scene with her powerful searchlights and so exposing the other ship as a poorly armed hulk. Never had light in darkness a more hopeful message than it had for those nurses, and when the stranger sheered off and was lost to sight, the nurse who had occupied my bunk came out and joined the others. The cruiser kept a parallel course with us for a while, then, with an assurance that we would not be troubled again, went off.

Dawn broke with the cries of children and the shouts of women all over the ship; the primary needs of mankind being emphasised as they rushed about looking for food, water and closets. The ship's galley was only big enough for the requirements of the crew; to provide extra fires we pierced five gallon drums with ventilating holes to serve as temporary stoves. The refugees fed on black bread and salami. A limited supply of tinned milk was available for mothers and babies. The single fresh water pump, hand driven, was in constant demand.

The medical staff was totally inadequate for the occasion; three doctors and six nurses to attend to 2,500 people. The doctors were dazed at first by the enormity of their task, but they never flinched and stuck it right through till the end. We had improvised the smoking-room into some kind of a hospital but it was altogether too small to be of much use. The Communist nurse was by now a harassed overworked woman. At sight of me she turned on me with such furious wrath and with such a flow of language that I was spellbound. She spoke so fast that I could not follow her, but I gathered she was blaming me, the chief engineer, for the deplorable conditions on board ship.

During the course of the day the wind freshened from the North-west, making for a heavy sea in which the ship rolled violently and reducing her speed. The doctors became apprehensive of the cases of measles and pneumonia that had developed overnight. They asked the captain to proceed to the nearest port. La Pallice was close at hand, and the captain agreed to take the ship there. He had had a worrying trip himself; the more ignorant and aggressive of the women were making wild threats to throw him overboard.

We dropped anchor at La Pallice in the evening, the refugees being by then reduced to a pitiable state, what with sea sickness, cuts and bruises, short rations and little rest. All the more welcome was the sight of a launch boat approaching with fresh provisions, bread, fruit and milk. Several sick persons were taken to hospital, including babies suffering from measles and a very old lady. She had been hoisted on board at Santander in her bath chair, and since then she had not moved from her chair, secured as it was against the engine-room casing. A girl, presumably her granddaughter, never left her. Not that the shrivelled old lady required much attention, for she was oblivious of her surroundings, her great sunken eyes shining yet empty of expression, staring all the time out to sea. She had collapsed the previous night, and was given an injection.

The next morning was spent by the crew in washing down the decks, cleaning up housings, and straightening things out generally. Meanwhile, the captain tried to get permission to land the refugees at La Pallice instead of at St. Nazaire, our original port of destination. All day was spent sending telegrams and making phone calls to Paris and London, but the French Government would not entertain the idea. Finally, the authorities being adamant, we hove anchor and proceeded to sea.

The refugees had by now regained some of their lost spirits and had found their sea legs; the decks were clean and the plentiful supply of fresh provisions gave them hope of better times ahead. The fine sunny day had mellowed into a beautiful evening, the moon shining clear on calm waters, with the friendly lights of the French coast twinkling in the distance. Everything conduced to put the refugees in a better state of mind and body, and the prospects of landing in the morning caused the younger ones to stay on deck and chatter far into the early morning. A group of young girls gathered in the warmth of the stokehold fiddley and sang Spanish songs; they had left everything they held most dear to them behind, but that did not crush the spirit of youth that rose in high hope to the future.

Tomorrow looked good to us all, but I little suspected when I turned in after midnight of the exciting sequence of events which were to take place before daybreak. The first alarm was at 2am when the captain banged on my door shouting, "Fire". I tumbled out of my bunk and scrambled over the bodies packed in the alleyway, my thoughts racing ahead of 2,500 people in a fire at sea. Soon we had the pumps working full bore and the hose playing on the fire in the forehold. Here an electric cable had chafed and set fire to a blanket. Fortunately, the fire was got under control before it had a chance to spread.

There was further commotion at my door when the mate burst in with the startling information that, "Spaniards taking charge of the engine room". On this occasion I could get nowhere near the engine room door on account of the number of excited people crowding round it, so I made my way down to the stokehold by way of the fiddley grating and ladders. No one was in the stokehold when I got there, but in the engine room I saw the firemen prowling around the platform armed with shovels and spanners. One of them said to me, "I don't think there is any more of them here". The engineer of the watch came down the engine room ladders, and to my enquiries he said, "Three Spaniards came out of the tunnel. I didn't know if they were wreckers or just plain stowaways so I chased them on deck. They did not want to go and I had to follow them up." The Spaniards, all young men, had no right on the ship and they were roughly handled by the women on deck.

The captain and I decided to sit the rest of the night out, and we were having coffee and biscuits when excitement turned to a confinement. Preparations were hastily made in the captain's dayroom for the new arrival, and everything went as well as could be expected under the circumstances. It was just one of those tragedies of the war that the baby's father had been killed in the fighting near Santander.

We arrived at St. Nazaire early in the morning to find crowds lining the docks. They were a silent crowd, however, and some of the refugees expressed disappointment, but, as with other refugee ships, the rumour went round that typhoid fever was rife on board. Disembarkation took four hours. Relays of doctors stood by the gangplank to inspect the women and children as they came ashore, being particular to examine necks and shoulders. Bottles of milk, and more fruit, were given to each child.

After the preliminary examination the refugees were led into the near-by shed for a more thorough inspection. Then began the business of dispatching them to the various towns. The women had their choice as to where they wished to be sent; some went to Belle Isle, old internment camp for English prisoners in the days of the Napoleonic Wars, and some even so far as Mexico. The French people were really good to these unfortunate victims of a civil war in which the majority had no part, even to parting in the streets with their own clothing in necessitous cases. A collection had been made in the schools of St. Nazaire for the benefit of the refugees. The nurses came round to wish me good-bye, not knowing then that they were coming back with us to take the last batch of refugees from Aviles. The Communist nurse stood beside me as the last of the refugees entrained for their several destinations. She might have been beautiful in happier days but that hate had eaten into her soul and had hardened the whole expression of her face. Only once had I ever seen her show any sign of womanly feeling, and that was when she was telling me of the sufferings of her people in Bilbao. It was then her voice faltered, and a tear swelled in her eye to fall and linger on her cheek.

Now, as she watched her kinsfolk go out into a strange world, she turned to me again with fire in her voice, and said, "Why don't you English come in now? You can't escape it, it's your turn next."

I do not know the dates in relation to this voyage by the *Pilton*, however, it is to my knowledge that she dashed into Aviles on July 27 and subsequently carried another batch of refugees out to France.

On July 22 the *Macgregor* under the command of Captain Owen 'Corn Cob' Jones was to have another run in with the Nationalist cruiser *Almirante Cervera* off Northern Spain. On that date the *Macgregor* left Santander with over 2,000 refugees on board destined for the French port of Pauillac. On leaving she was signalled to by the *Almirante Cervera* inside the three mile limit, to stop. Captain Jones took no notice, and the cruiser then fired two warning shots across the Welsh merchantman's bows. Again Captain Jones ignored the order from the Nationalist to stop, whereupon two more shells were fired across her bows. 'Corn Cob' Jones never faltered for a minute and steamed at full speed for international waters, knowing full well what fate was likely to befall his cargo of unfortunate Basques if he were to submit to the insurgent warship. All on board were plainly relieved when the *Macgregor* cleared territorial waters and came immediately under the protection of H.M.S. *Kempenfelt* which was waiting off the port and had witnessed events with great concern. As a result of this the captain of the *Almirante Cervera* immediately represented to the British Naval Authorities that the *Macgregor* in not obeying the order to stop had taken advantage of his humanitarian feelings, but that she would not take further action. It is true that the cruiser could have sunk the *Macgregor* if she had wanted, but Captain Jones did not care a hoot, he had done what he was paid to do, and fulfilled his obligation to the now exiled Basque Government.

Two days later, on July 24 the *Backworth* also left Santander with a couple of thousand refugees also destined for France.

On that same day the Welsh managed steamer *African Trader* entered territorial waters off Gijon fully intending to make that port to embark more refugees, however she was ordered to stop by the insurgent cruiser *Baleares*. The British ship ignored this instruction, and what looked like a dangerous incident was rapidly getting out of control. Seeing the situation from outside the three mile limit H.M.S. *Escapade* went up as far to the ship as she was allowed and signalled for her to come out of territorial waters. The *African Trader* complied with this and thereafter came under the protection of H.M.S. *Escapade* and H.M.S. *Royal Oak*. The latter vessel sent a boarding party to the merchantman to check that she was bona fides, and then escorted her back to the safety of St. Jean de Luz. However the British merchant ship was not finished, and she did eventually make it into Gijon.

Later that day the British steamer *Mirupanu* which was also making for Gijon was captured off Gijon inside the three mile limit by the insurgent ship *Ciudad de Valenica*, and thereafter escorted to Ferrol for examination and enquiry.

On July 27 the Hong Kong registered steamer *Marion Moller* was turned back off Santander. She had been chartered by the National Joint Committee for Spanish Relief and was carrying £500 worth of food and £700 worth of medical supplies. The medical supplies consisted of a quantity of anti-gas gangrene serum, specially requested by the Republican authorities, anaesthetics, and anti-typhoid serum. Again, the following day she was blockaded off Gijon. But eventually she made it into a Northern port with her much needed cargo.

Meanwhile the attacks on merchant ships in the Mediterranean continued, both inside and outside territorial waters. Ships were being bombed, machine gunned and in some cases even torpedoed. Losses were heavy, but mostly at this stage by other nationalities than British. On July 24 the Newport registered steamer *St. Quentin* was damaged by aircraft bombing at Valencia. Her plating was damaged in No. 1 hold and about 200 tons of her cargo of sugar was lost. However, she was able to leave port, and effect repairs later in the United Kingdom.

On July 27 the steamers *Sarastone* and *Tuskar Rock* were able to leave Gijon with thousands of refugees without interference by the insurgent navy. On July 29 there were actually three ships blockaded off Santander awaiting an opportunity to make a dash for port, these were the steamer *Marvia*, the British ship *Bobie* which was owned by a relative of Thomas McEwen, and was actually registered at Gibraltar, and the tanker *Valetta* owned by Jas German and Co. Ltd., Cardiff, and which was subsequently renamed *Arlon*. All three eventually broke the blockade, but which ports they managed to enter, I do not know, other than the *Bobie*, which made Santona near Santander.

Such was the concern of the Admiralty concerning the situation off Northern Spain, that they felt it necessary to actually define Spanish territorial waters. As a result the Board of Trade made the following announcement to British shipowners, on July 30.

> Owners and masters of British vessels should note that, as a working arrangement for the purposes of the present emergency only, territorial water off Santander and Gijon are to be regarded as extending to three sea miles from:
> (a) In the case of Santander, a line from Cape Ajo to Cape Lata.
> (b) In the case of Gijon, a line from Cape de Torres to Cape San Lorenzo.

These arrangements actually extended the three mile limit somewhat, but it made it easier for merchantmen and the Royal Navy alike to know their respective positions exactly.

Although Bilbao had fallen as early as June 19, the British Government had prior to that date, even with this situation existing between British merchantmen and the insurgent Navy, been involved in secret negotiations with General Franco to ensure that when the port fell they would still secure continuity of supplies from the iron ore mines. Resulting from the negotiations General Franco agreed to allow sixty per cent of the iron ore production to be exported to Britain. The Italians and Germans were very angry about this agreement. When Hitler and Mussolini had come to Franco's aid, Germany had been allowed a substantial part of the minerals being exported through Huelva, and had expected similar treatment regarding the Northern deposits, particularly in view of the support being given to the Nationalist Cause.

Whilst British ships were involved in confrontation with Nationalist forces off Northern Spain between Santander and Gijon, other shipowners resumed trading to Bilbao to load iron ore quite happily, and almost oblivous to the events being enacted a little way off to the West. Constants (South Wales) Ltd resumed carrying supplies on behalf of G.K.N. and other owners quickly followed. Franco, would not, however, allow any ship to enter Bilbao, if it had previously traded with Republican held ports during the conflict.

On August 3 the Board of Trade made the following announcement regarding the situation at Bilbao.

> The following information in regard to the conditions of shipping at Bilbao, based upon information obtained from the Naval Authorities in control of that port, has been reported by His Majesty's Ambassador at Hendaye: There are no mines or other obstructions in the channels leading to the port of Bilbao, but pilotage is compulsory for all vessels. British vessels are required to give 72 hours' notice of their arrival in order to enable berthing to be allotted and due notice to be given to the Pilotage Authorities. This notice should be sent to the Naval Authority at Bilbao or to Captain Caveda, the Officer-in-Command of the region. The Naval Commandant at Bilbao will allot the berth and vessels must conform exactly with his order. The local Spanish Naval Authorities state that merchant vessels which have been trading with ports under the control of the Spanish Government will not be allowed to use the port, except that in case of *force majeure* they may enter the port, though they will not be allowed to remain more than 24 hours.

This announcement meant in effect that if a shipowner had used one of his ships in the Republican or Basque cause, that ship would be prevented from docking, but if he owned another ship which had not gone to such ports that ship would not be disallowed.

Returning to the situation further to the West, on August 11 the British steamer *Caper* was captured by the Nationalist vessel *Tritonia* off Cape Vidio and taken under escort to Rivadeo for examination and enquiry

On August 12, in view of the tens of thousands of Spanish refugees which had been entering France on British ships, the French Government announced that in future:

> No Spanish refugees will be allowed to land in France, unless disembarkation in France has been authorised by the French Government in each individual case.

They specifically requested the British Government to inform immediately the masters of British vessels concerned with the carriage of refugees from Spain. France, being sympathetic to the Republicans, had done more than most, but they were now declaring that they could not take any more. However, they did in fact take more, and many were resettled outside France. Britain had always made it known that no ship would be allowed to bring refugees to the United Kingdom, but they played their part by taking some of those which had transited via France. The announcement was ignored by British shipowners, who continued to evacuate refugees from Northern Spain right up until the fall of the last ports in October 1937.

On August 16, two Welsh ships left Northern ports with refugees, totalling 5,600 in number, with complete disregard for the French announcement. The Cardiff steamer *Nailsea Vale* from Aviles and the Newport registered *Bramhill* from Gijon. Neither was intercepted by insurgent forces, and all their unfortunate passengers were subsequently disembarked in France.

On August 25 Santander and Santona fell. The insurgent forces actually taking Santander whilst Santona was taken by Italian troops. Alfred Pope's ships figured heavily at this time as the *Seabank* and *Kenfig Pool* were at Santander while the *Seven Seas Spray* and the chartered *Bobie* were at Santona. All four had been chartered by the Basque Government to carry refugees to France, but had been caught in port before they could embark due to the confusion existing. Because Santona was taken by Italian troops the Basque representatives there actually managed to negotiate to evacuate thousands of their countrymen on the ships. Permission was granted on August 27 to the master of the *Bobie*, a Frenchman, Georges Dupuy, and a Non-Intervention Observer on the *Seven Seas Spray*, Costa e Silva, a Brazilian, for the embarkation to take place. However, General Franco was soon to intervene to stop the ships leaving, and the following day all were taken off and marched down the quay, some for imprisonment and many for eventual execution. Thereafter the *Bobie* was allowed to leave, and she quickly set off for France with seven stowaways on board. However, Captain W.H. Roberts was not allowed to follow with the *Seven Seas Spray*, probably being the price of breaking the blockade of Bilbao in April, and the ship and her crew were detained in the port. Alfred Pope was luckier with the *Seabank* and *Kenfig Pool* as they were allowed to leave Santander on September 2 and made for a French port.

Numerous air attacks were now concentrated on Gijon, and on August 27 the four ships in the port were damaged by bombs. These were the Welsh managed *African Trader* which started taking in water forward as a result of the damage, the Jack Billmeir ships *Stanwood* and *Stanbridge*, and the Moller Line's *Hilda Moller*. The masters of these ships now considered that the ports of Northern Spain were too dangerous and the *African Trader, Stanwood* and *Hilda Moller* sailed from the port without delay. The *Stanbridge* was unable to weigh anchor due to the damage, but managed to leave on September 11. The worst damaged ship was the *African Trader* commanded by Captain Bullock. Such was the concern that H.M.S. *Fearless* and H.M.S. *Foresight* were sent to accompany her in case she should founder on route to La Pallice. The damage was so bad, that her pumps were only just able to keep her afloat, and on arrival at the French port she had to be beached immediately to prevent her from sinking. She was subsequently refloated, drydocked, and following repairs sailed about a month later for Cardiff.

Having safely left Gijon on August 16, the *Bramhill* re-entered the war zone on route from Brest back to Gijon, when on August 28 at 6pm she was sighted by two insurgent trawlers near the port. The insurgents considered that the Welsh ship was inside territorial waters and fired a warning shot to order her to stop. The master of the *Bramhill* did not consider he was within territorial waters and refused to stop, as a result a further shot was fired across her bows. Again she refused to comply. At that stage H.M.S. *Fearless* arrived to investigate and after an exchange of signals it was confirmed that the *Bramhill* was still outside the three mile limit, and she was allowed to proceed (to seaward) and the incident was closed.

Following the success of his land forces General Franco was able to tighten his blockade of Gijon and Aviles as the Nationalist fleet under the cruiser *Almirante Cervera* had a much shorter length of coastline to patrol. As a result, even the ever persistent *Thorpehall* returned to Bayonne on September 7 having been prevented from entering Gijon.

Meanwhile attacks continued on ships in the Mediterranean, and on September 2 the British tanker *Woodford* was attacked by a submarine (obviously Italian) on the surface, which torpedoed and sank her in international waters whilst she was on route to Valencia with 10,000 tons of petrol from Constanza. Of her crew, all were Greek, with the exception of a Hungarian radio operator, a Rumanian cook and a British control officer. Eight members of the crew were injured and one killed.

At 10pm on September 8 the Billmeir steamer *Stanwold* was captured by an insurgent vessel within territorial waters off Rivadesella, within sight of H.M.S. *Resolution*. The *Stanwold* had been observed outside the three mile limit by the British warship, which had warned her that she was approaching territorial waters. Almost immediately after she crossed the three mile limit an insurgent torpedo boat which had been hovering on the horizon, gathered speed, overtook the *Stanwold* and fired three warning shots. The *Stanwold* altered course and proceeded accompanied by the torpedo boat, in the direction of an insurgent port. When asked by H.M.S. *Resolution* if he had anything to report, the master of the *Stanwold* wirelessed, "I am captured."

However, the Royal Navy were not exactly happy with this turn of events, and it was certainly their belief that the merchant ship, having been paid to carry the cargo in advance had actually allowed herself to be captured, by arrangement as it were, in order to sell the cargo to the Nationalist forces. I leave the reader to judge for himself.

A number of ships flying the British flag, particularly tankers, which appeared to be manned by complete crews of foreign origin, were captured during this period in the Mediterranean.

After repeated representations from the British Government, on September 10 the Welsh steamers, *Molton* owned by Lord Glanely and which had been captured on July 14, and the *Candleston Castle* which had been taken by Nationalist forces on July 17 and which was owned by Reginald Jones, were released, and allowed to leave Spanish waters.

Both ships made for Bordeaux, where they communicated with their respective owners.

On that same day the Claude Angel steamer *Hillfern* which was making for Gijon, was attacked by an insurgent armed trawler when about 35 miles off the coast. Although shelled she was not hit, and she immediately turned away from the Spanish coast. Shortly after she was machine-gunned by aircraft, which appeared to be trying to hit her deck cargo of drums of oil. The ship was undamaged in the incidents. The *Hillfern* arrived at Bayonne on September 12 to await developments and further instructions from Cardiff.

On September 15 the Billmeir steamer *Stanmore* which had set out from La Pallice for Rivadesella to pick up refugees was attacked by aircraft, which fortunately missed. She continued to sail Westwards along the Spanish coast, but decided to turn back when a shore battery opened fire on her. Undamaged she put back to Bordeaux arriving on September 16.

On October 3 the steamer *Bobie* which was carrying a cargo of foodstuffs from Antwerp for either Aviles or Gijon was intercepted off the coast and taken into Rivadeo, and later taken to Ferrol where she arrived on October 6. This ship had been allowed to leave Santona a month earlier when that port fell to the insurgents. She did not carry any British crew members whatsoever, but was owned by Mr. W.H. McEwen of Parkston, Dorset, who was related to Thomas McEwen the partner of Alfred Pope, the by now famous Welsh shipowner engaged in the Spanish trade. The ship was registered at Gibraltar and was flying the British flag, and was actually chartered in by Alfred Pope who had re-chartered it out to the Republican Government.

On Tuesday, October 5 two British ships were captured off Northern Spain. The London registered *Dover Abbey* was not in territorial waters, but unfortunately was not in sight of British warships who would have acted to rescue her in these circumstances. She was carrying a cargo of maize and dried peas from Antwerp for Gijon, and was manned by a crew of nineteen of which thirteen were British; her master was Captain A.E. Jackson of London.

The insurgents must have had great pleasure in taking the other ship that day, as she was none other than the *Yorkbrook* which they had captured once before and lost. Last time she flew the Estonian flag but now she was flying the British flag and was registered at Swansea under the ownership of Claude Angel. She had been chartered to the Spanish Government to carry refugees from Gijon to Bordeaux, and was trying to enter Gijon at the time of her capture.

As the net closed around Gijon and Aviles the passage of British merchantmen to and from these ports became more dangerous. Not only were they being hampered by the Nationalist Navy but they were now equally as likely to be attacked from the air or shelled by the shore batteries.

On October 20, the day before Gijon fell, the Billmeir ship *Stangrove* with nearly 600 refugees on board was captured just after leaving the port by an armed trawler. However it became clear that the ship had made it to international waters and on the arrival of H.M.S. *Southampton* on the scene she demanded that the merchantman be released. The commander of the cruiser *Almirante Cervera* released the vessel under protest, and thereafter the *Southampton* escorted her from the war zone.

Finally the war in the North came to an end on October 21, 1937 when Gijon, Musel and Aviles were taken by the Nationalists.

Six days after the taking of the last Northern stronghold by General Franco's forces the Billmeir steamer *Stanray* was intercepted by an armed trawler outside the three mile limit off Aviles. What she was doing no one knows, but being outside territorial waters, the Royal Navy responded to her distress call and released her.

With the war in the North over General Franco gradually allowed the British ships captured by his forces, to be released. The *Molton* and *Candleston Castle* were released a month earlier, and the others followed: –

Name	*Date Released*
Seven Seas Spray	1.11.1937
Stanwold	1.11.1937
Caper	12.11.1937
Mirupanu	13.11.1937
Bobie	13.11.1937
Dover Abbey	15.11.1937
Yorkbrook	20.11.1937

The only Briton on the *Caper* had been the master and the *Mirupanu* carried none at all.

During the detention of the *Caper* at Ferrol an incident occurred between the six armed guards put on board the ship and members of the crew, and three were shot dead, a Dutchman and two Russians. The master Captain Cossintine was wounded with a bullet in his chest, and was treated ashore. He later returned to the ship but subsequently handed command over to a relief sent out by the owners.

This manning of British flag ships by foreign nationals was a point that both the Nationalist and Royal Navies were acutely aware of. It transpired that foreign owners were transferring their ships to the British flag in order to obtain a measure of protection from the Royal Navy, which no other navy had undertaken to do. The Admiralty were less than pleased to be seen protecting foreign nationals sailing foreign owned ships but flying the British flag. This resulted from temporary certificates of British registry being granted, in many cases by British Consuls abroad. A tightening of the rules was surely called for.

7. ATTACKS IN THE MEDITERRANEAN

Such had been the situation in the Mediterranean, with ships being attacked by submarines, aircraft and occasionally by a surface warship, and the claims and counter claims that Italy was primarily responsible, that on June 23, 1937 both Italy and Germany had withdrawn from the Naval Patrol in the Mediterranean. Portugal soon demanded the withdrawal of British observers from their frontier with Spain, and on July 12 France withdrew the facility from her border, which was in fact closed anyhow. The attacks continued, and the cost to Russia, particularly, was so great that she informed the Republican Government that whilst supplies would continue to be provided that in future Spain would have to arrange the shipping to carry them. This resulted in an even greater participation by British flag vessels, as more and more they were sent to the Black Sea to load for Spain. However, the overall effect was to reduce the supplies reaching the Republic.

Britain and France were so concerned by the attacks in the Mediterranean that on September 6 all States with Mediterranean frontiers together with Germany and Italy, but excluding both sides in the Spanish conflict, were invited to attend a Conference to be held at Nyon in Switzerland commencing on the 10th. Germany and Italy proposed that the matter should be dealt with by the Non-Intervention Committee, but this was unacceptable to Britain and France. In the end Hitler and Mussolini boycotted the conference, but the result was to see decisions made whereby France and Britain would jointly patrol the Mediterranean, and that any unidentified submarine, warship or aircraft whether inside or outside Spanish Territoral Waters would be liable to be attacked by the British and French forces. Subsequently Italy at her own request asked to join the patrol. This agreement did not solve the problem associated with attacks by the two warring Spanish parties, but this was the risk that merchant shipowners had to reconcile themselves with, and few withdrew from the trade because of it.

Whilst to some extent when dealing with the events of the North Coast I gave details of ships in addition to the Welsh owned vessels, I will try where possible to confine myself to the Welsh ships with regard to the conflict in the Mediterranean.

The Royal Navy were very concerned to be seen to be doing their duty properly. For some time past they had suspected that British ships were on occasions carrying war materials to the Republic in direct contravention of the Merchant Shipping (Carriage of Munitions to Spain) Act, 1936. As a result on occasions British ships were taken into port and examined in detail. One such ship to be examined was the Cardiff managed steamer *African Mariner* which was intercepted in the Eastern Mediterranean whilst bound from Odessa and Novorossisk to Barcelona. The Admiralty had suspected for some time that the owners of this ship were engaged in gun-running, and had watched her movements with great attention.

Having been stopped by H.M.S. *Greyhound* an armed guard was put on board and the vessel escorted into Valetta Harbour, Malta, arriving on November 19.

Much of the *African Mariner's* cargo of salt fish and sulphate of ammonia was discharged, but rods were used to probe the wheat in her deep holds. After ten days of exhaustive searching by the Naval Authorities in Malta nothing was found and the vessel was allowed to sail with her much needed cargo, and subsequently arrived at Barcelona.

Whilst the British Naval forces were examining suspected ships in the Mediterranean, General Franco's forces were still stopping neutral flag vessels in the Straits of Gibraltar, and taking them into Ceuta for examination. A number of vessels and/or cargoes were confiscated by the Nationalists when it was found that a vessel had a cargo destined from or to a port held by the other side in the conflict.

Late in December that veteran of the Spanish Civil War, the Newport steamer *Bramhill* was lying at Burriana when the Nationalist Navy shelled the port. Several shells hit the Welsh ship but amazingly little damage was caused and no injuries suffered by the crew. The *Bramhill* left the port for Marseilles where she was examined and a report passed to Claude Angel, but repairs were deferred until a later and more convenient time.

Following the release of the steamer *Seven Seas Spray* by Franco's forces at Santona on November 1, 1937 Alfred Pope decided to rename the ship before sending her back to the Spanish war zone. As a result she was given the new name of *Seabank Spray* appropriately reflecting his interest in the Porthcawl hotel. On January 16, 1938 the ship was lying at Burriana when three insurgent aircraft attacked the port, and a bomb fell within 200 yards of the vessel. This ship's luck continued to hold out as again she suffered only very minor damage.

Many of those neutral ships being intercepted off Ceuta by insurgent naval forces were actually on route from Welsh ports with cargoes, often of coal, for Republican ports and elsewhere. Two Estonian ships were intercepted and their cargoes confiscated at Ceuta before being allowed to leave. These were the *Juss* on January 21 and the *Pomaron* a day later, both were on passage from Cardiff, the former to Barcelona and the latter vessel to Valencia.

On January 31 the British steamer *Endymion* was torpedoed and sunk in the Mediterranean by what must have been an Italian submarine. There was outrage felt in Britain and Spain at the heavy loss of life, which accounted for eleven people, including the master, his wife and the second engineer. As a result of the quick action of the Republican authorities the remaining members of the crew were speedily rescued. The Royal Navy stepped up their patrols following this incident.

Claude Angel's steamer *Bramden* was lying at Sagunto on February 25 when six rebel seaplanes made a determined attack on the vessel in the port. One bomb actually landed on the ship's oiltank but fortunately failed to explode. Three members of her crew including the wireless operator, Mr. G. Garrod, were wounded by shrapnel, but thankfully none seriously.

On March 15 the *Stanwell* owned by Jack Billmeir's Stanhope Steamship Co. Ltd., and commanded by a Captain Davies of Cardiff appears to have been the target for an insurgent air attack whilst lying at Tarragona. In the raid the ship was severely damaged and her forecastle was completely gutted. Of her complement, two men, Messrs Mulholland and King, both from Newport were killed, as was the Danish Non-Intervention Control Officer. Four other members of the crew were seriously injured. Two months earlier the London steamer *Thorpeness* had been bombed at this port with the loss of seven members of her crew, including A. Perrott of Barry.

Clearly these attacks on British ships were designed to hamper supplies to Republican ports, by dissuading owners from sending their ships into ports where considerable danger existed, and to interrupt the actual cargo working on the ships themselves. Clearly the insurgents felt that the disabling of a ship was a bonus which obviously supported the main objective. The air attacks on Republican ports had been intensified considerably.

Another veteran of the Spanish conflict, Claude Angel's steamer *Hillfern* was attacked on April 17 while lying at Carthagena. Although there were no casualties among her crew, the ship had suffered damage to her shell plating, lifeboats, bridge and accommodation from the air attack. After making temporary repairs she proceeded to the safety of Algiers arriving on April 24 for a fuller examination to be made.

On April 25 four British ships were damaged at Valencia during an insurgent air attack. These were the Blue Star Line's *Celtic Star* with one killed and three wounded, the Billmeir ship *Stanland* with the death of one of her crew, and the Claude Angel vessel *Fredavore* and Stone and Rolfe's *Isadora* . All were fairly badly damaged by bombing. The *Isadora* was actually outside the harbour when she was caught by the insurgent aircraft, and after the raid was towed into the port and quickly unloaded. All the ships survived and eventually were able to proceed from the port.

During an air attack on Barcelona on May 12 two ships were damaged, the Pelton Steamship Company's *Zelo* and the Cardiff managed *African Mariner*. The *Zelo* suffered one member of her crew critically injured when a bomb fell on the quay, twenty yards from the ship. The *African Mariner* was moored next to the *Zelo*, and a Greek galley boy was slightly injured in the face by small fragments of shrapnel. Damage to the Welsh ship was confined to the wireless operator's cabin, the wireless aerial was cut down from the mast and she received three large holes in her funnel.

Shortly after, Claude Angel's by now famous ship, the *Yorkbrook* was damaged at Valencia when a bomb fell on the quay near her. There were no casualties on board, although her bridge and lifeboats were slightly damaged. She was however, able to proceed without making repairs.

On May 22 the Barry Shipping Company's (later to become the South American Saint Line) steamer *St. Winifred* was bombed and damaged at Alicante whilst unloading a cargo of foodstuffs. There were no casualties at that time and the damage to the ship was reported by her master as:

> Main condenser inlet and fresh-water distiller fractured, starboard side engine-room deckhouse, port side poop deckhouse, fiddley deck, all bridges, decks sprung, boats concussion strained, starboard boat holed, all inside accommodation woodwork amidships broken, bridges woodwork shattered,

telegraph, electric lights, wireless damaged, shrapnel perforations over all, much small damage, wood fiddley deckhouse shattered, fresh water tank damaged. Can effect temporary repairs.

However, she was not so fortunate on June 6, as during two insurgent air attacks on Alicante she was so badly damaged that she was in danger of sinking. In these attacks five crew members were killed, Engineer Halliday, Seamen Hennessey and McMillan, the mess-room boy and the cabin boy. As a result she was eventually towed to Marseilles where she was subsequently declared a constructive total loss, and in November was sold to Italians who after carrying out repairs placed her into service as the *Capo Vita*. Richard Street, the managing director of the owners was so sickened by this casualty that he immediately withdrew from the Spanish trade.

The Welsh managed steamer *Penthames* was lying at Valencia towards the end of May when she was the subject of a number of air attacks. On the 20th four bombs landed near the ship, but damage was slight. Two days later she received a direct hit during another raid. The Master Captain Cochrane and second mate were interviewed by reporters:

Captain Cochrane alleges that the 'planes bore German markings, and he adds that a telegram of protest had been sent to London. He recalled that on the previous Friday (May 20) four bombs had burst in the vicinity of the vessel. Mr. Brown, one of the officers stated that three bombs were dropped and that in his opinion, the vessel was aimed at. Two bombs, he said, burst 45 feet from the vessel, and the third struck the deck, making an enormous hole and destroying the cabins of the officers and engineers. Two officers, Graham and Oglesberg, received a number of wounds, and a Chinese boy had his legs torn and his shoulder dislocated. A fire broke out in the vessel but was rapidly got under control by the crew and the harbour officials.

The ship was again to be the subject of air attacks on May 25 and 31, and as a result of the latter she sank at her moorings in the port. Fortunately no one had lost his life, although the attacks had been heavy. During the attack on Valencia on May 25 our old friend the *Thorpehall* was caught at anchor just outside the port and was sunk by the insurgent attack. Of her crew five were wounded including three who lived at Cardiff.

The Mooringwell Steamship Company's ship *Jeanne M* was moored at the Coal Quay at Barcelona on May 29 when she was damaged by bomb splinters and concussion from an air attack on the port. The ship suffered damage to her hull and superstructure, which was subsequently repaired at Barry. At the time of the attack she was discharging a cargo of coal and generals from South Wales.

Republican territory was cut in two when Franco's troops reached the Mediterranean in April 1938. The first major port in the region to fall to the Nationalists in this determined thrust, was Castellon on June 15. This level of activity by the Nationalist forces saw an increase in attacks and prior to its fall Castellon was subjected to a heavy aerial bombardment. The Stone and Rolfe steamer *Isadora* was badly damaged by an attack at 1am on June 9, when three bombs struck the vessel. Damage consisted of her bridge, cabins and engine room being wrecked and the following day the ship sank. There were fortunately no casualties in the attack. At the time she had been unloading a badly needed cargo of wheat which she had brought from Marseilles.

After taking Castellon the insurgents subsequently raised the *Isadora* and after repairing the ship placed her under their own flag under the new name of *Castillo Frias*. Prior to the fall of the port her crew had been conveyed from the war zone by the Royal Navy.

This division of Republican territory presented a major problem to them and to those, who by now were virtually all British, who were prepared to carry their supplies. Indeed transport between the two regions held by the Republic was also carried on British ships. By now the supplies reaching the government were being transhipped at Oran or Marseilles from vessels not prepared to run the gauntlet, into other ships, of which the Welsh owned and managed were predominant. These ships ran a feeder service into Spain, and obviously taking great risks were handsomely rewarded. The instances of damage were far more numerous than had previously been the case.

8. FREDERICK JONES AND COMPANY

In relation to the Civil War British shipowners were actually earning enhanced freight rates to engage in the trade. After almost fifteen years continuously depressed freight rates, it was difficult to keep out of a trade which was likely to yield some handsome returns. Many historians have asserted that owners were earning double their normal profits. I contend that this is not so, they were actually earning something like double their gross freight. Simply defined this meant that a profit of say £200 on a freight of £2,500 prior to the civil war or on a voyage not connected with the trade, returned on a voyage to or from Spain during the conflict something like £2,700 on a gross freight of £5,000. Clearly the returns were very good. The expenses of running to Spain were greater than other trades, but this was only marginally so, and usually related to war risk and increased crew insurance and to crew war bonuses. This left considerable profit for the owner prepared to enter into the trade. Whilst owners were prepared to risk their ships it is clear that seafarers were also prepared to take the risks associated with the trade, and who could blame them after such unemployment as was experienced in the depression of the early 1930s.

Many commentators have asserted that usually old ships were employed in the trade thus leaving greater profits for owners. This is partly true, old ships were used mostly, but that was because of the war risks insurance which on an old ship with low capital value was fairly reasonable. However, the employment of new tonnage which incurred the penalty of high insurance premiums was entirely prohibitive to owners. The only gains therefore were to be found by using older tonnage.

In my book *The Abbey Line* (1983) I included a chapter on the Spanish Civil War, and because this is the only company of which I have a detailed account of each vessel's voyages and earnings, I hope that readers will excuse me for quoting from it at length.

> In consequence of Frederick Jones' decision to enter this trade, the *Neath Abbey* was chartered to the Nederlandsch Bevrachtings Hantoor and loaded foodstuffs at Rotterdam commencing on April 8, 1937 the freight for this was £3,612 12s 1d and whilst on voyage charters payment was usually made on discharge of the cargo, Frederick Jones had no experience of this trade or the charterers, and before agreeing to carry this cargo insisted that payment was made in advance on completion of loading. For this purpose his younger son, Herbert Stanley Jones went to Rotterdam to receive the payment. The ship thereafter sailed and completed discharge at Alicante on May 1. The profit made on the voyage outwards was £2,369 3s 5d and represented what the ship had previously taken over a year to earn. At noon on May 1 a freight was accepted for the ship, and she proceeded in ballast from Alicante to Valencia where she commenced loading fruit on behalf of the Golden Cross Line. This cargo was completed by moving around the coast and taking on further parcels of fruit at Castellon and Burriana before she set out for Liverpool where on

discharge being completed she proceeded in ballast to Port Talbot where she arrived on May 22. The freight for this homeward passage had been £2,481 yielding a profit of £1,664 19s 2d.

Referring back to chapter 4 for a moment, it will be remembered that the *Melrose Abbey* had carried a cargo of pyrites from the Nationalist held port of Huelva to Dublin in April, 1937. On completion of discharge she ballasted across to Rotterdam where her next voyage was to be for the Republican side.

On May 2, 1937 the *Melrose Abbey*, not yet a year old commenced loading foodstuffs at Rotterdam for Valencia on behalf of the Lamorna Shipping Co. Ltd at a freight of £4,100. On arrival at Valencia the ship was delayed before her cargo could be unloaded and as a result demurrage for 4 days 3 hours was paid to the firm at the rate of £50 per day, i.e. £206 5s 0d. The ship then proceeded in ballast to Sfax where a cargo of phosphate, not connected with the Spanish trade was loaded at a freight of £2,441 14s 4d for Rotterdam.

On May 23 the *Neath Abbey* commenced loading coal at Port Talbot for the Lamorna Shipping Co. Ltd which was destined for Cartagena. The freight involved was £4,313 12s 10d and on entering the Mediterranean the ship had to call at Gibraltar to collect representatives of the Non-Intervention Committee for which purpose the firm was refunded £6 2s 6d port charges. Thereafter the ship discharged at Cartagena and proceeded to Sfax where she loaded phosphate at a freight of £2,511 4s 8d for Nantes. She then proceeded in ballast to Flushing for bunkers, arriving on July 16.

On June 20 the *Melrose Abbey* commenced loading another cargo of foodstuffs at Rotterdam for the Nederlandsh Bevrachtings Hantoor for a £4,698 1s 11d freight destined for Alicante and on discharge proceeded in ballast to Phillipville (French North Africa) where iron ore was loaded for Grangemouth (freight £2,423 7s 5d) and after unloading she went in ballast to Immingham, arriving on August 8.

The Spanish (Republican) Authorities were having difficulties in obtaining woodpulp in which to pack fruit for export abroad, and as this fruit represented a major part of the economy, they tackled the search for pulp with some urgency. As a result on July 17 Herbert Stanley Jones was sent by his father to join the *Neath Abbey* at Flushing, and with him on board the ship passed through the Kiel Canal out into the Baltic, and then anchored at Hernosand in Sweden.

When I wrote *The Abbey Line* book, I failed to include an interesting account given me by Herbert Stanley Jones. This concerned the German Pilot who navigated the ship through the Kiel Canal. The master of the *Neath Abbey* was a fluent Welsh speaker named Jones, and everyone on board the vessel was surprised to hear the Pilot conversing with him in Welsh. This was due to the fact that in Germany at that time it was a condition that before qualifying all master mariners had to have some experience under sail, and the Pilot had obtained part of his by sailing on a Cardigan ketch. Returning to the voyage:

At this time he (H.S. Jones) was in conversation with the Spanish Commercial Attaché in Sweden and a Swedish National – Mr. Axel J. Ahlstrand, and

Claude Angel's "Sunion" was bombed and sunk off Valencia on June 22, 1938.
(York Collection)

The "Dellwyn" was sunk at Gandia on July 27, 1938. She is shown under her earlier name of "Madge Llewellyn".
(York Collection)

Another view of the "Madge Llewellyn" which later became the "Dellwyn".
(Welsh Industrial & Maritime Museum)

The Guardian Line steamer "Maclaren" was formerly Frederick Jones' "Singleton Abbey".
(Welsh Industrial & Maritime Museum)

Another view of the "Maclaren" of Cardiff.

(York Collection)

Jas. German and Co. Ltd., Cardiff, managed the steamer "Becheville" (seen under her earlier name of "Newton Elm") which was engaged in the Republican trade.

(York Collection)

Claude Angel's "Bramwell", although engaged in the Spanish trade, escaped damage.
(York Collection)

Claude Angel's "Kaolack" was bombed and damaged at Valencia on November 25, 1938.

David Barnett's steamer "Cemenco" was also bombed and damaged at Valencia on November 25, 1938.
(John Clarkson)

The steamer "Atlantic Guide" was bombed and damaged at Valencia on February 9, 1939.
(Laurence Dunn)

The Dillwyn Steamship Company's "Bellwyn" refused to submit to a Nationalist warship off Southern Spain on March 10th, 1939.

The steamer "Transeas" was damaged by bombing in February and March, 1939. She is shown under her earlier name of "Polmela".

(R. M. Parsons)

The steamer "Ronwyn" was engaged in the Spanish trade. She was owned by the Dillwyn Steamship Co. Ltd.
(Laurence Dunn)

The Dillwyn Steamship Company's steamer "Josewyn".
(Welsh Industrial & Maritime Museum)

Stone and Rolfe's "Glynwen" was damaged during the conflict.
(York Collection)

A striking view of the "Philipp M" owned by the Mooringwell Steamship Co. Ltd. of Cardiff.

(Laurence Dunn)

negotiated a freight for a cargo of woodpulp from the Swedish Mills at Utansjo and Bollsta destined for Valencia of £6,850 (profit £4,937 15s 8d). At this time it was arranged for the ship to be taken on time-charter to the Spanish Government directly, on her return from the Mediterranean. The *Neath Abbey* proceeded to Valencia without incident and quickly unloaded and then proceeded to Bona to load a part cargo of iron ore, completing at Bizerta, and then set off for Middlesbrough where her cargo was discharged on behalf of Scott Bros. Ltd at a freight of £2,626 5s 3d.

On August 11 the *Melrose Abbey* commenced loading coal at Immingham for Rafferty and Watson Ltd (freight £4,193 1s 10d) and set out for the Mediterranean where she discharged her cargo at Tarragona. On completion she proceeded in ballast to Casablanca where on September 9 she started to load phosphate for Sas van Gent (freight £2,237 17s 11d).

The *Neath Abbey* having completed unloading a cargo of iron ore at Middlesbrough in September, 1937 sailed in ballast for Sweden and on September 15 at 5pm having anchored at Hernosand was taken on time-charter by the Spanish Government at £4,750 per month. Initially the ship was employed carrying woodpulp from Utansjo and Bollsta to Valencia, then carrying a cargo of fruit from Almeria to Gothenburg and Stockholm, and then another cargo of woodpulp from Sweden to Barcelona and Valencia. It is interesting to note who made the payments for this time- charter. The first monthly payment made in advance was by the Moscow Narodny Bank, then the next three months by the Oficina Commercial Espana and thereafter by the Mid Atlantic Shipping Co. Ltd., a company in the United Kingdom set up by the Republicans to organise shipments via ships under the British flag.

Having discharged a cargo of phosphate at Sas van Gent during September, 1937 the *Melrose Abbey* was sent in ballast to Finland where she loaded woodpulp at Rauma and Spjutsund (Kotka) at a freight of £6,850 for the Spanish Commercial Delegation and discharged it at Valencia. After this she proceeded in ballast to Sfax where on October 20 she commenced to load a cargo of phosphate for Nantes (freight £3,508 6s 3d). She then proceeded to Rotterdam where a cargo of generals was loaded for Howard Tenens Ltd (freight £5,225) which was discharged at Barcelona. The ship then went back to Antwerp in ballast where a cargo of pig iron was loaded to the account of Howard Tenens Ltd. (freight £5,700) for Sagunto. The ship then proceeded to Valencia where on January 14, 1938 she commenced loading fruit for T.A. Finzi, Layman and Co. Ltd. (freight £4,378 6s 8d). Having taken a part cargo she moved on to Gandia to complete her cargo and then sailed for London. Having unloaded she ballasted across to Rotterdam where a cargo of barytes was loaded (freight £747 16s 7d) for Garston, whence she moved around to Swansea in ballast to load coal on behalf of Cory's Trading Ltd. (freight £4,754 6s 3d) for Barcelona.

During February, 1938 Frederick Jones and Company took delivery of the first of two new ships on order at the yard of William Gray and Co. Ltd., West Hartlepool, and her first voyage was as follows.

This new ship was immediately sent to Sunderland where she loaded a cargo on behalf of Atkinson, Prickett Ltd. This consisted of 3,736 tons 9 cwt. of coal at

25/- per ton, totalling £4,651 12s 6d, and 15 tons 3 cwt. of generals at the same freight – £18 19s 6d, destined for Barcelona.

The fact that the Russians were no longer willing to send ships to Spain meant that the Republicans were anxious to obtain ships to bring cargoes from Odessa in the Black Sea on their behalf. Knowing that the *Neath Abbey* was in a Spanish port in January, 1938 they informed Frederick Jones and Company that they intended to send the ship in ballast to Odessa to load for the Mediterranean Coast of Spain. Frederick Jones was none too pleased with this, as he feared that they would use the ship to carry armaments. However, his insurance had been paid on the basis of 10/- per cent, and this only allowed for trading as far East in the Mediterranean as Malta. Frederick Jones did his best to wriggle out of letting the ship carry out the voyage, but finally had to relent when his crew expressed their willingness to sail her, and when the Spanish offered a one off payment of £2,500 over and above her monthly freight of £4,750. This was to cover the extra cost of insurance, additional war bonus and bunkers which the firm would have to buy in Russia. When bought in 1934 the *Neath Abbey* had cost £7,500, and during the Spanish voyages she had been insured for £10,000 at 10/- per cent, costing £50. However, Frederick Jones had to pay at the rate of £8 per cent to insure the ship for this voyage, making a total of £800 for her £10,000 valuation.

The ship sailed East to the Black Sea on January 31 where she fortunately took an age to load her cargo at Odessa (whilst there she was out of harm's way). She was at this time commanded by a very experienced Abbey Line master, Captain Jones, who on emerging back out into the Mediterranean skirted the North African coast and slipped into Oran on March 11 to wait his best opportunity for a passage across to Spain. He waited for five days and on March 16 in darkness slipped across to the safety of Aguilas a Republican held port where he waited for a day before slipping up the coast again under the cover of darkness into Valencia where the ship took over two weeks to unload her cargo of generals.

Meanwhile the two newer Abbey ships, *Melrose Abbey* and *Margam Abbey* were en route for Barcelona where they had docked early in March. On the night of March 16 Mussolini had ordered his air force to bomb Barcelona, and during the next two days a total of eighteen attacks were made on the city and its port with a resulting heavy loss of life. Fortunately the two new Abbey ships were undamaged, but while the *Melrose Abbey* was covered by war risk insurance throughout, the *Margam Abbey* still on her maiden voyage was subjected to such considerable delay that her cover ran out whilst the ship was in the port. The cost to obtain cover for his brand new ship in a port subject to enemy attack was almost impossible, but eventually he achieved it, but had to pay the sum of £2,735 12s 10d. The freight for this voyage had been £4,670 12s 0d, added to which demurrage for 11 days 3 hours at £30 per day – £333 15s 0d was paid by the Mid Atlantic Shipping Co. Ltd. Thus the profit which should have been considerable was reduced to £202 0s 11d.

It was apparent that the employment of a new ship in the trade was totally uneconomic from that point onwards, and Frederick Jones immediately set about withdrawing the two ships, *Melrose Abbey* and *Margam Abbey*. The *Melrose Abbey* was sent to Casablanca in ballast where on March 30 she commenced to load phosphate for Sas van Gent (freight £1,467) and following discharge ballasted back to Cardiff, arriving on April 12. Having paid such a high price to re-insure the *Margam Abbey* he decided to get a last cargo out of Spain with the ship. Thus on March 20 she left Valencia and moving along the coast loaded fruit at Denia, Alicante and Cartagena for the London River at a freight made up of 180,000 cu.ft. @ 30/- per 100 cu.ft., plus demurrage for 4 days 2 hours at London at £30 per day = £122 10s 0d. (Profit £767 12s 6d). This homeward cargo was for the account of J.A. Finzi, Layman and Co. Ltd. On completion of discharge at London she made her way in ballast to Cardiff where she arrived on April 16.

Frederick Jones and his sons were very glad to see their two new ships and their loyal crews safely home, and the *Neath Abbey* was redelivered to the firm at Marseilles on April 4 on completion of her eventful time-charter. She was then sent to Sfax to load phosphate for Nantes before returning to Cardiff on May 2. The *Neath Abbey* had received some damage to her funnel during an air attack and she and the *Melrose Abbey* each spent a month at Cardiff for repairs and overhaul.

The new *Margam Abbey* after her eventful voyage was still only two months old and did not require any attention. Therefore she was quickly loaded for an outward passage to the Mediterranean, but I hasten to add, not for Spain.

In June, 1938 the second of the two ships on order at West Hartlepool was completed, and was given the name *Tintern Abbey*.

However, although he had paid for the ship, Frederick Jones decided to leave her moored at West Hartlepool. When in the Spring of 1938 he had withdrawn the two new ships *Melrose Abbey* and *Margam Abbey* from the Spanish Republican trade, this was because they were too modern to provide anything like a realistic return as the war risks insurance had become prohibitive. However, there were no such penalties to be incurred in trading the *Neath Abbey*, as she had only cost £7,500 in the first place, and had virtually paid for the new ship anyway. Therefore the *Neath Abbey* was returned to the trade to Spain where she proved so successful in running the blockade. Meanwhile the new *Tintern Abbey* was left at West Hartlepool, unregistered, almost like a car in a showroom. She could not start to erode her four year gap to her first survey as she had not yet been registered. She was paid for, and was not burning any holes in the founder's pocket. The ship she was due to replace was earning in a month what the new ship would take a year to earn in the way of profits, and Frederick wisely decided to leave well alone as the Spanish trade would not last for ever.

Thus after spending a month at Cardiff for repairs the *Neath Abbey* sailed from the port on June 2, 1938 in ballast for Havre where she loaded general cargo on behalf of Howard Tenens Ltd. (freight £3,500) and set off for Valencia. The rate had dropped since her last voyage but the shippers Howard Tenens Ltd agreed to pay the war risks insurance which was back to 10/- per cent. The profit for this outward passage totalled £1,192 0s 1d. On June 28 having discharged at Valencia she quickly proceeded to Sfax where she loaded phosphate for Sas van Gent.

After this the *Neath Abbey* was employed on a Kara Sea voyage for twelve weeks, where she was joined by the *Margam Abbey*.

In October, 1938 the *Neath Abbey* was time-chartered to the Spanish Government or more precisely Messrs J.A. Finzi, Layman and Co. Ltd., the hire being 16/- on her deadweight, i.e. £3,200 per month. The ship sailed from Cardiff on October 8 for Antwerp where she loaded foodstuffs for Cartagena and Almeria and after discharge returned to Antwerp in ballast arriving on November 21. She was quickly loaded again and set out two days later. There is no record of the ports she discharged at in Spain on this occasion but on January 4, 1939 the ship was handed back to Frederick Jones and Company at Tunis.

The ship then carried a cargo of phosphate from Tunis to Granville and on completion was brought around to Cardiff where she arrived on February 9, 1939. Frederick Jones and his sons could see that the Civil War in Spain was all but over. The ship was quickly sold, and her replacement, the *Tintern Abbey* was now commissioned. The *Neath Abbey* had provided some of the firm's greatest profits with a single ship, and between the period from July 23, 1934 to February 9, 1939 her total freights were £109,555 16s 10d yielding a profit of £45,000.

Thus the Abbey Line withdrew from the Spanish trade about twelve weeks before the conflict ended, but it is worth noting that although the *Neath Abbey* had received some minor damage, not one of their ship's had actually figured in a casualty report due to the hostilities. A magnificent record.

General Franco kept his promise not to allow ships that had traded with the Republic to enter Spanish ports, as in the early part of the Second World War the *Melrose Abbey* was refused entry to Valencia where she had been directed by the British Ministry of War Transport to lift a cargo. As a result the firm had to divert the *Tintern Abbey* to get this cargo. It was as well that she had been left at her moorings until the civil war had ended.

9. REPUBLICAN TERRITORY DIVIDED

The fall of Castellon on June 15, 1938 gave the insurgents a base in between the Republican held territory, and eventually they pushed further to the North. The increase in air attacks was alarming to many of the British merchant ship masters, and as a result, even before the fall of Castellon seven of them had lodged a protest with the British Consul on June 10 concerning the air attacks on their vessels at Barcelona. This protest was forwarded to the Foreign Office in London. It was made by Captain Nesbitt of the steamer *Gothic*, Captain C. Lewis of the *Stanburn*, Captain A. Still of the *Hamsterley*, Captain Lamb of the *Sea Glory*, Captain Jones of the Welsh owned *Alex*, Captain G. Davies of the *Stanbrook* and the master of Pope's *Kenfig Pool*. Two of these ships were real veterans of the war having survived from the blockade of Bilbao, over a year earlier.

However the attacks continued; on June 15 all the British ships moored at Barcelona were badly shaken by an air attack on the port. Another veteran of the blockade in the North, the Guardian Line's *Macgregor* received damage to her bridge in this attack, but was able to leave the port without undergoing repairs.

On the morning of the following day a seaman named Edgar Marquet of the *Seabank Spray* (ex *Seven Seas Spray*), that ship of Alfred Pope's which had actually broken the Bilbao blockade, was killed in a raid on Barcelona. He had left the ship when the alarm was sounded and was running for an air raid shelter when a bomb burst near him. He died in an ambulance on the way to hospital. The ship was undamaged in this raid. In these air raids other British ships had suffered damage.

On the morning of June 22 the Cardiff managed steamer *Sunion* was lying one mile outside Valencia when she was struck by two incendiary bombs. In the attack one bomb fell forward and one amidships, wrecking the bridge and setting her on fire. The vessel sank, but before this her crew of 32 and a German Non-Intervention officer were taken off, uninjured. The ship had been in ballast at the time and due to dock at Valencia in order to pick up passengers.

Later that day the *African Trader* was intercepted on the high seas off the coast of Spain by an insurgent seaplane, which circled round her and wirelessed the master ordering him to proceed to the Nationalist held Palma, Majorca. As a result the ship sent out a distress message which was intercepted by H.M.S. *Imogen*. The Naval vessel went to her aid, and the seaplane made off. Subequently the *African Trader* arrived at Valencia having been escorted to the three mile limit by the *Imogen*.

On June 27 the British steamers *Lalcham, Bramden* (Claude Angel's), and *Stanwold* were damaged by flying shrapnel during a raid on Alicante, in which the British steamer *Farnham* was sunk.

On the same day the Welsh managed tanker *Arlon* was set on fire while lying at Valencia. The ship received one direct hit which set her on fire, while another bomb fell between the ship and the quay, and a dozen bombs fell alongside the quay near to the vessel. During this attack a member of her crew, a Rumanian was killed, and another was injured. At the time she had been discharging a cargo of 7,000 tons of aviation spirit from St. Louis, Rhona, although all but 100 tons had been unloaded. Such was the danger that the burning ship was towed out of the port and eventually sank off Nazaret Beach, one mile South of Valencia. When interviewed by the press the second officer gave this account.

> Planes dropped forty bombs in a straight line along the wharf, fifteen of them falling on the wharfside, one hitting us flush and another falling between us and the dock. We were due to sail in half an hour's time, as the vessel had been discharging since Saturday (June 25) and had only 100 tons of cargo left.

On July 10 the Belgian non-intervention officer on board the *Yorkbrook* was injured by flying shrapnel during an air attack on Valencia. A number of ships were hit by shrapnel, but no damage was caused. One bomb actually fell right between the steamers *African Trader* and *Yorkbrook*.

A number of Welsh ships were turning up during this period asking for surveys due to previously unreported bomb damage in Spanish ports. On July 18 the Stone and Rolfe steamer *Glynwen* arrived at Gibraltar reporting damage in Spanish ports through bombing both in April and June 1938. The vessel was described as generally strained, slight leakage in her hold, peaks and engine-room.

Following her bomb damage at Barcelona in June, on July 19 the *Macgregor* turned up at Rouen where she was surveyed, and the following reported: starboard lifeboat chocks destroyed, all wood decks found leaking, five port lights broken, one ventilator tube destroyed, sun deck over bridge leaking, wireless and dynamo out of order, deck water service pipes damaged, auxiliary piping on deck damaged, sanitary tank leaking and other sundry damage. It was not too unusual for a ship damaged by bombing, if she was still seaworthy, to make for a port out of the war zone to effect repairs.

The Welsh ships *Dellwyn* and *Bramhill*, both under the control of Claude Angel of Cardiff, were unloading at Gandia on July 22 when the port was raided at 11am and 50 bombs fell 200 yards away from the ships, which fortunately were undamaged. However the *Dellwyn* was to be the target for virtually constant attacks by the insurgents over the next five days, whilst the *Bramhill* had left the port after the first attack. The *Dellwyn* was struck by bombs and machine-gunned on the 25th, 26th and 27th, and on the latter date within a few hundred yards of a British warship she was finally sunk by a direct hit on the vessel. At the time the crew were ashore, and there were no casualties. After the conflict was over this ship was refloated by the Nationalists, on May 10, 1939 and following repairs was placed in the Spanish merchant fleet as the *Castillo Montesa*.

The steamer *Kellwyn* formerly 'Potato' Jones' *Marie Llewellyn* was one of a number of ships damaged by an aircraft attack on Valencia on July 28. Two men were killed in the attack the Danish Non-Intervention officer and the Chinese cook whilst the ship suffered a number of small holes above her waterline and smashed doors and furniture in the accommodation. The mate and three other seamen were also wounded in the attack. The ship was unloading a cargo of coffee and sugar at the time.

Such was the level of air attacks on Republican held ports that air raid shelters had been erected in port areas. When an air raid commenced the stevedores, dock workers and ships' crews would quickly leave the ships and take refuge. Indeed some ships crews were actually housed ashore, where possible, away from the most dangerous areas, when cargo was not being discharged. This constant volume of air attacks created long delays and congestion in ports, and instead of ships being able to discharge their cargoes in days or up to a week, the time in port was extended in cases up to two or three weeks. This made the job of carrying cargo to and from the Republic even more dangerous. The majority of ships engaged in the trade were now operating what amounted to a feeder service from Marseilles and Oran, whilst ships not prepared to take such risks were discharging at those ports instead of running the gauntlet. One aspect of the crews leaving their ships when an air attack was imminent was that those casualties amongst the crews were often killed and injured on the quays whilst running for cover.

The British Government made repeated protests to General Franco about these air attacks, although it was clear that in addition to insurgent aircraft, German and Italian forces were also involved. In one reply General Franco published a list of vessels which, he claimed were British and had been carrying munitions for the Barcelona Government. It was claimed that since January 1, 1937 more than 200 ships flying the British flag had attempted to carry contraband to Barcelona Government ports. The same reply also mentioned the names of a number of companies which it claimed were engaged in the arms traffic to Spain. Franco stated:

> Britain has an easy remedy to stop the bombing of her merchant vessels, this is by prohibiting the use of the British flag to protect the undignified contraband traffic in arms in the Republican zone. Nobody doubts the final outcome of the war. Why try to lengthen Republican resistance?

The majority of British ships (and Welsh) were lawfully engaged in carrying cargoes of foodstuffs and other materials, and lifting fruit for export from the Republic and since the date quoted indeed about 200 British ships had been trading to the Republic, but they were not all, if any, engaged in carrying arms. The British Government, had given strict instructions that the Royal Navy were to keep a close eye on this aspect, and whilst no doubt a few took a chance, it was very isolated.

The Burgos or Nationalist Government went on to list British ships which it alleged were engaged on carrying munitions to the Republic.

> *Orange* – Left Marseilles on April 30 for Barcelona with explosives. (No such ship listed in Lloyd's Register).

> *Bramhill* – Left Marseilles on April 30 for Barcelona with shells and cartridges. (Ship owned by Bramhall Steamship Co. Ltd., managers Claude Angel and Co. Ltd. Ship registered at Newport, Monmouthshire.)

Fenja – Left Marseilles on April 30 for Port Mahon, Minorca, with munitions and provisions. (Swedish vessel.)

Isadora – Left Marseilles on May 21 for Republican Spain with munitions. (Ship bombed and sunk on June 9 at Castellon.)

Kellwyn – Left Marseilles on May 21 with munitions for Republican Spain. (Ship managed by Claude Angel, Cardiff.)

Muneric – Left Odessa for Barcelona and passed through the Bosphorus on April 25. Despite an investigation at Palermo (Italy) it unloaded at Barcelona five planes, 935 light machine guns, 24 heavy machine guns, 149 lorries, and rolls of barbed wire. (Ship owned by Counties Ship Management Co. Ltd., London.)

Gripfast – Left Amberes for Almeria with armoured plates and barbed wire. (Ship owned by the Newbigin Steam Shipping Co. Ltd., Newcastle.)

Dover Hill – From Russia to Alicante, passed through the Bosphorus April 30 with 200 lorries and 400 tons of war materials. (Ship owned by Dover Steamship Co. Ltd., and registered at Glasgow.)

Marklyn – From Newcastle to Gibraltar, thence left for Republican zone May 5 with barbed wire and long cases. (British owned.)

Stanburgh – Left Amberes for Valencia May 15 with cargo suspected to include 20 million cartridges. (Ship owned by the Stanhope Steamship Co. Ltd., London, Manager J. A. Billmeir.)

Latymer – Flying the British flag, owned by a Greek and chartered by Republican agents, with other ships flying the Greek flag plying between Odessa, the Piraeus, and Marseilles, passed the Bosphorus on May 15 with lorries and accessories, and picked up at Piraeus cartridges, shells, and tanks for Valencia. (No such ship listed in Lloyd's Register.)

Dover Abbey – Left Gibraltar for Alicante on June 3 with Russian tanks camouflaged as lorries, and munitions, all shipped at Le Havre. (Ship owned by Anglo-Iberian Co., London.)

The statement also gave a list of British companies which it said were shipping materials to Republican Spain.

Stanhope Company, which owned only two ships before the Spanish war; and today owns nineteen.

Billmeir Company, which organised the Stanhope Company, and formed five other companies for the same trade. These (it claimed) were the Westcliff Shipping Company, Thameside Shipping Company, Veronica Steamship Company, Dillwyn Steamship Company, and Trent Maritime Company, all of which were formed after the Spanish war started. The name of the Mid-Atlantic Company was also given.

In relation to the shipping companies Franco had almost got it right, other than the fact that Billmeir did not have a financial interest in the latter five. He did however, act in most cases as cargo brokers for all of them. Clearly the allegations about specific ships were rather wild. The Admiralty would never have allowed a British ship to call at Gibraltar with munitions. They were actively inspecting a great number of British ships to ensure that any allegation, such as this one, were without foundation.

Reaction to the insurgent statement was swift. Claude Angel of Cardiff, who managed both the *Bramhill* and *Kellwyn* stated.

> The *Bramhill* and *Kellwyn* have been carrying coal and general cargo for the Barcelona Government. The *Bramhill*, I believe, is at Almeria. The *Kellwyn* is carrying a cargo of wheat.

I think that this statement is probably a true account of the ship's employment. I would however refer readers to the statement in R. Gonzalez Echegaray's book quoted earlier.

Another South Wales shipowner was quoted by the *Daily Mail* at the time as saying.

> General Franco is very well informed as to the nature of the cargoes leaving British ports for Spain. He has an agent in every port and he is watching the departure of all vessels. Ships engaged in carrying shells and ammunition are owned mainly by foreigners.

Mr. Edward R. Newbigin, the 75 year old Managing Director of the Newbigin Steam Shipping Company was quoted as saying "It's a wicked lie" in reply to Franco's allegations that the *Gripfast* was carrying armour plates and barbed wire to the Barcelona Government, Mr. Newbigin continued.

> This ship has never loaded any cargo in any French port for Spain. She has been to Spain a few times but never taken anything but coal, coke or foodstuffs on the outward journey, and she has generally brought back fruit.

Most of the cargo being carried to Republican Spain was consigned in British ships, of which a considerable number were owned and/or managed in South Wales. The Republicans were still receiving arms and indeed someone was carrying them. I leave readers to form their own opinion.

Meanwhile on August 15 Mr. R.A. Amery, the wireless operator of the Welsh ship *Hillfern* was killed on the quay during one of four successive air raids on the port. On the same day the British Non-Intervention observer on the *Fredavore* was wounded when he was hit by shrapnel. Neither of the ships was damaged in the attacks.

On August 20 Alfred Pope's *Seabank Spray* was attacked at sea off the Spanish coast by Italian aircraft which dropped bombs near the vessel which fortunately missed. The ship made port without damage or casualties.

Barnett's ship *Lucky* was subjected to an air attack on September 1, whilst lying at Aguilas, but she only received minor damage. Although casualties ashore were heavy, no one was injured on board.

The *Seabank Spray* and the *Bobie* were at Barcelona on September 13 when two squadrons of insurgent aircraft attacked the city. Both ships received damage from shrapnel and concussion. Captain Johns of the *Bobie* and his Dutch chief engineer received cuts and bruises in the attacks, whilst two men on the quay were killed. The damage was not severe enough to prevent them from sailing when their cargo had been discharged.

During September, 1938 survey was carried out on the Welsh steamer *Nailsea Lass* at Barry in respect of previously unreported damage which had been sustained by the vessel being bombed at Valencia on January 6 and subsequent dates, and at Cartagena on July 12. This ship which was managed by E.R. Management Co. Ltd., of Cardiff, was repaired at Barry and thereafter resumed trading, although I have no information as to whether she went back to Spain or not.

On September 16 a number of British ships were damaged during an air atttack on Barcelona. The *Stanlake* was seriously damaged by a bomb which exploded on the poop. The *Bobie* was slightly damaged by shrapnel, the Greek cook M. Athanasy being injured in the head. The *Seabank Spray* and *Lake Hallwil* which were both at anchor were slightly damaged in the attack.

The *African Mariner* and the American *Wisconsin* received some damage at Barcelona on September 24 when a bomb exploded in the water fifty yards from their stern. There were no casualties on board the ships, but in the raid five people were killed on shore and 21 injured.

On October 3 the *African Mariner* still at Barcelona, was not so lucky. As a direct hit was recorded on the vessel. The bomb ploughed its way through two decks and exploded in her cargo of wheat blowing out the bulkhead. There were no casualties. Her master was Captain P.H. Manley of Penarth. Apparently the cargo of wheat had cushioned the impact of the explosion as the ship was not that seriously damaged.

On the following day a number of British ships were damaged in an air attack at the port, including the *Gothic, Thorpebay, Lake Hallwil* and Claude Angel's *Hillfern*. Nobody was injured, and the Welsh ship was only superficially damaged.

On October 9 Claude Angel's steamer *Bramhill* was lying at Barcelona when she was hit by a bomb and set on fire when an insurgent seaplane raided the port at about 10pm. The bomb tore an 8 ft. hole in the vessel's deck amidships. This direct hit damaged the cabin of the mate and the second officer. Fragments of the bomb were scattered over a large area of the vessel, while two other bombs, one of which fell on the quay and the other in the sea, also caused damage in the form of small holes in the hull above the waterline. It was thought that the bomb might have sunk the vessel had not the explosion spent all its main force in the coal bunker. The master, Captain Thomas Parker and the crew were ashore at the time of the bombing. The explosion caused steampipes to burst and consequently put the winches out of commission for a while, resulting in delays in the discharging of her cargo, which consisted of beans and beef.

At Valencia on October 10 the steamer *Transit* managed by David P. Barnett of Cardiff was hit by a bomb during one of three insurgent air attacks on the port during the night. The ship was unloading a cargo of coal from Oran at the time and was extensively damaged. The deck and superstructure were badly holed and buckled but fortunately there was no damage below the waterline, and no danger of the vessel sinking. Owing to an early alarm the crew had gone ashore to refuges before the bomb fell. This ship was actually Lord Glanely's old *Molton* which had been captured by the Nationalist cruiser *Almirante Cervera* on July 14, 1937 off Santander and released on September 10 of that year. She had been sold to the Continental Transit Co. Ltd., of London in 1938 and placed under the management of David P. Barnett of Cardiff under the name *Transit*.

The Barnett managed steamer *African Explorer* and another British steamer, the *Lake Hallwil* were badly damaged during a heavy raid on Barcelona on the morning of October 19. The Welsh managed ship received a direct hit when a bomb passed through her deck, exploded in her cargo of wheat and made a large hole in her side above the waterline. Three of her crew, all foreign, were wounded as a result. Subsequently the ship completed the discharge of her cargo and made for a port outside the war zone for survey and temporary repairs.

General Franco's forces were getting more daring. He sent an armed merchant vessel, the *Nadir* into the North Sea in order to intercept Republican Merchantmen which were trading outside the war zone. It came as a shock to the world to hear that on November 2, 1938 the *Nadir* had intercepted and shelled a Spanish merchant ship, the *Cantabria* off Great Yarmouth. Although this incident was outside British territorial waters it was virtually in sight of Great Yarmouth itself. The ship shelled the *Cantabria* for about two hours commencing at 2pm. Of the 37 on board the merchantmen, including three women and five children, the majority were taken on board the *Nadir* and the steamer *Pattersonian*. However, the *Cantabria's* master, Captain Manuel Arguelles, his wife, two children and the second steward were rescued by the Cromer lifeboat.

The British Government were most concerned by this event which was extending the conflict, now to the shores of the United Kingdom itself.

When the civil war broke out, there were many difficulties experienced by those serving on Spanish merchant ships. The owners of these ships were domiciled in both zones of Spanish territory, and the crews were often of different political persuasions, this resulted in ships not wanting to return to one or other of the different zones, a. because the owner lived in another, and b. because the crew or part of the crew were of another zone. In some cases crews actually refused to sail the ships and in others the owners refused to allow them to proceed to one or other of the zones. Many Spanish ships were moored in different parts of the world, some staying in port throughout the conflict. Others continued sailing, but staying away from Spain itself, and finding employment in the general tramp trades. In cases of ships being under Nationalist control, the Republican Government took action through the courts to seize the various vessels and take over the control of their movements. In effect they were quite lawfully able to nationalize any Spanish ship not controlled in Republican held territory. Many Spanish ships tried in the early days to make it to their home ports in Spain, usually Republican held with cargoes, and these were often attacked in International Waters by Nationalist warships and captured or sunk. There were cases recorded of Spanish merchantmen being chased into French waters and shelled and sunk, to the horror and displeasure of the French Government, in their own territorial waters. Protests were made and threats made to the insurgent forces.

The result of these attacks and the clear dangers in which Spanish merchant ships found themselves was to see fewer and fewer of them putting to sea. A considerable number were laid up in the United Kingdom. This was one of the major reasons why such a large proportion of the cargoes taken to and from Republican held Spanish ports was carried in British ships.

Our old friend the *Yorkbook* was the victim of yet another attack, when on November 6 she was damaged by an air attack whilst lying at Almeria in ballast. No casualties were incurred on the ship, but a number of rivets were started, although this was only of a minor nature. She subsequently made for Oran for survey and repairs, and then loaded for Valencia.

Reginald Jones' *Candleston Castle* was the subject of an air attack at Barcelona on November 12 during which little damage was caused by the flying shrapnel, but two members of crew were injured, Mr. N.W. James, the third engineer received a broken leg whilst fireman Ali Ahmed was slightly injured. Both were put ashore into hospital and the ship eventually left port without them.

At about this time the *African Explorer* whilst at Cartagena received further damage which necessitated her proceeding to Marseilles where repairs were carried out. On November 23 Alfred Pope's *Kenfig Pool* was one of three ships slightly damaged during an air attack at Barcelona. On that same day our old friend Claude Angel's *Bramhill* was slightly damaged at Barcelona, but in all these cases no casualties were suffered amongst the crews.

On November 25 four British ships were damaged by shrapnel when five three engined insurgent aircraft dropped 50 bombs on Valencia. These ships were the Billmeir ship *Stanwold* and the Welsh managed *Bobie, Kaolack* and *Cemenco*.

Four British ships, including the *Transit* and *African Mariner* managed by Barnett of Cardiff were slightly damaged in an air raid on Barcelona on December 5. The Nationalist forces were intensifying their bombardment of the Catalan Province, and it is truly amazing to me how the same ships were being damaged time and again. It is clear that these ships were running a very risky and efficient feeder service to the Republican ports from Oran and Marseilles, and that their cargoes of mostly foodstuffs were badly needed by civilian populations barely existing on what must by now have been a starvation diet. No one would pretend that the shipowners were motivated by any idealogical ideals, but having been involved in many cases with supplying the Republican side from the start of the conflict, albeit for handsome returns, it is surely to their credit that they didn't desert them now when the going was getting rough. It was definitely getting very dangerous in the South and South East of Spain.

Another Barnett managed vessel was the victim of an insurgent air raid on December 28 at Valencia. This was the *Emerald Wings* which was struck by a bomb which caused considerable damage. Three of the crew were injured in this attack. Back in Barcelona, the *Transit* was one of three ships slightly damaged when shrapnel from bombs landing on the quay hit them on January 4, 1939. Ten days later the Welsh steamer *Bellwyn* was struck by shrapnel during an air raid on Valencia, but she was little damaged.

Nationalist forces had taken Tarragona on January 15, 1939, and were finally to capture Barcelona on January 26, and thereafter resistance in the Catalan Province was soon crushed. However, before the fall of Barcelona, some of the veterans of the Spanish Civil War were to be found, as in the Bilbao and Santander campaign, hanging on to the very last minute still supplying the port. The last weeks in Barcelona were to be extremely costly to Welsh shipowners.

The *Seabank Spray* was at Barcelona on January 21 when she received a direct hit on her cargo of coal, but was only slightly damaged. The *African Mariner* was damaged amidships during a raid the following day. This ship was unloading a valuable cargo of wheat and frozen meat. On January 22 the old stalwart of the civil war *Yorkbrook* was hit and sunk by a bomb which exploded and holed her below the waterline. The *African Mariner* was again struck by bombs on this day and as a result four Greek members of crew killed. Such was the damage that she sank in the port on the 23rd. The steamers *Huntress* and *Dover Abbey* were also badly damaged in this period. The former ship had received fourteen holes in her hull forward but fortunately they were all above the waterline.

Further attacks on Barcelona on January 24 and 25 resulted in even further damage to vessels in the port, including bombs hitting the *Dover Abbey, Thorpebay,* the French *Yolande* which sank as a result, the *Huntress* and *Seabank Spray*, and Claude Angel's tanker *Miocene* which was also sunk.

Barcelona fell to the Nationalist forces on January 26 and just before the city fell, in fact the day before, the surviving British ships although badly damaged left the port for Marseilles. It was obvious that Barcelona was doomed, but surprising that the ships had left it so late to make good their escape, as the last days at Barcelona had seen four ships lost in the port due to insurgent bombing. It was a bedraggled quartet of ships which docked at Marseilles, these were the London registered *Thorpebay*, the Gibraltar registered *Bobie* which was controlled by Alfred Pope, the legendary *Seabank Spray* which once again had been chancing her luck and the Barnett ship *Huntress*.

Thus with the fall of Barcelona another chapter of the civil war came to an end.

10. THE FINAL MONTHS OF THE CONFLICT

After the steamer *Seven Seas Spray* had reached Bilbao on April 20, 1937 the owner Alfred Pope had said, "General Franco is not going to keep a single one of our ships from going about its lawful occasions". He had carried out that promise, as the same ship, albeit now called *Seabank Spray* together with his chartered vessel *Bobie* and the other two ships only left Barcelona within hours of the insurgents taking the city. However, even Alfred Pope could see that the conflict was drawing to a close, and thereafter withdrew his damaged ships from the trade. Of the Welsh shipowners involved in the carriage of supplies to the Republican side, only two actually continued after Barcelona fell, these were David P. Barnett of Cardiff and the Dillwyn Steamship Co. Ltd., which had previously been managed by Claude Angel of Cardiff but was now being managed by Stockwood Rees and Co. Ltd., of 20-24, Pembroke Buildings, Cambrian Place, Swansea.

The remaining Republican territory now bordered Madrid in the West, Valencia in the North and Almeria to the South, and included Cartagena and Alicante.

Barnett's steamer *Emerald Wings* was damaged by an air attack at Cartagena on February 5 when five warplanes dropped fifty bombs on the town. This attack resulted in two members of the ships crew being killed, the cook John Philips and an Arab fireman. On February 9 Barnett's other ship, the *Atlantic Guide* was damaged by bomb splinters at Valencia, but no casualties were reported amongst her crew.

Whilst Majorca and Ibiza had fallen to the Nationalists on July 18, 1936, the smaller Minorca had remained strongly Republican. On February 9, 1939 the hand over of Minorca was negotiated and took place under the supervision of the Royal Navy, who evacuated the Republican troops by agreement just prior to the Nationalist occupation taking place.

Another Barnett ship the *Emerald Wings* was damaged during an air attack, when Cartagena was bombed on February 10, but no casualties were reported and little damage sustained. On that same day another of David Barnett's fleet, the *Lucky* was hit during an air raid at Valencia when a bomb exploded in her No. 1 hold. However, the ship did not live up to her name and quickly sank by the head, although fortunately there were no casualties on board. The steamer *Transeas* was also slightly damaged when an attack occurred on Valencia on February 26.

On March 8, 1939 the Nationalist Forces announced a blockade of all the Mediterranean coast Spanish ports, as follows:-

> The whole of the Mediterranean coast of Spain between Adra Sagunto is closed for navigation to all kinds of ships of whatever nationality and whatever kind of cargo; no ships should approach it without the proper authorisation of the Admiral in Chief of the blockade force of the Mediterranean within a distance of three miles. Any ship not observing these instructions will be

> seized. Navigators are warned that off the fortified base of Cartagena and along the stretch of coast between the Torre de Mesa Light and Cabo Palos there will be submarines with orders to sink any ship which attempts to approach the coast within the three mile limit, no matter what the nationality of the ship may be. Ships proceeding with cargo for other ports on the coast in the 'red' zone, whatever their nationality, should go to ports in liberated Spain, preferably Barcelona, Palma, Majorca or Malaga.

This in effect declared another blockade, but this time the war was all but over. However, there were a few Welsh ships left in the zone at this time.

At 9.32pm on March 10, the Welsh steamer *Bellwyn* gave out the following distress call.

> *Bellwyn*, position Cape San Antonio bearing 170 degrees; 23 miles distant; ordered to Palma, Majorca, by warship. Immediate assistance. Steamer *Stangate* under escort, proceeding Palma, Majorca. (remainder jammed.)

At 10.24pm the following message was sent by the *Bellwyn*, addressed to all British warships.

> Refused to submit, now left alone. Please rescue steamer *Stangate* being taken to Palma, Majorca.

Apparently the *Stangate* was en route from Valencia to Almeria to load a cargo of oranges destined for London, and was in company with the *Bellwyn* when they were both ordered to stop by a Nationalist warship. Both ships tried to make for the coast and evade capture, but the *Bellwyn* was more fortunate, as the warship concentrated her attentions more on the Billmeir ship. The *Bellwyn* had refused to submit, but the *Stangate* was captured by the insurgent ship. As a result of the *Bellwyn's* distress message the Royal Navy sent the destroyers H.M.S. *Intrepid* and H.M.S. *Impulsive* to investigate. They found the *Stangate* making for Majorca under escort of the insurgent warship, and immediately demanded her release, which they achieved without any incident or problems. The ship was then escorted to Gibraltar.

On March 29 Valencia fell to the Nationalists, and Madrid was also taken when the defending forces withdrew from their positions. On that same day the Cardiff managed steamer *Atlantic Guide* was approaching Valencia, blissfully unaware of the situation, and was subjected to machine gun fire from an aircraft. At the time she was negotiating to take on board refugees which she did in fact succeed in doing.

On March 30 the last ships to leave Spain, the *African Trader* with a thousand or so refugees, and the Billmeir ship *Stanbrook* with 1,800 departed from Alicante. The last stronghold of Republican resistance Almeria, Cartagena and Alicante fell to Franco's forces on March 31, and the civil war officially ended on April 1, 1939.

11. CONCLUSION

Of the ships engaged in the trade to Republican Spain twenty-seven ships flying the British flag were sunk, of which nine were owned and/or managed in South Wales. A number of the Welsh ships were refloated by the Spanish authorities after the end of the conflict and thereafter placed under the Spanish flag, as follows:

Vessel	*New Name*
African Mariner	*Castillo Montjuich*
Dellwyn	*Castillo Montesa*
Isadora	*Castillo Frias*
Lucky	*Castillo Benisano*
Miocene	*Castillo Pedraza y Campanero*
Yorkbrook	*Castillo Monteagudo*

Whilst the blockade of Northern Spain was undertaken by the insurgents and a number of actions took place in which the Royal Navy had to intervene, there was a measure of understanding between the respective naval forces as to each other's positions. It is to the Nationalists credit that not a single British life was lost at sea due to the blockade. The same obviously cannot be said for the conflict in the Mediterranean but those actions at sea where British lives were lost were in my view mainly as a result of Italian intervention. The bombing attacks in port resulted in the greatest loss of life and was due to insurgent aircraft heavily supported by German and Italian forces.

The conflict had lasted for a total of thirty-three months and the participation of British merchant ships had clearly helped to stiffen Republican resistance. Without the supplies carried by these ships the civil war would have ended far earlier; Franco was well aware of this, and frequently complained about it.

Most of the Welsh merchant ships which survived this conflict were to be lost in the Second World War which commenced five months later. Alfred Pope sold his ships and withdrew from shipowning altogether. His famous *Seven Seas Spray* passed to the Mooringwell Steamship Co. Ltd., of Cardiff and as their *Jeanne M* (not to be confused with their earlier ship of that name damaged in the civil war) while on a voyage from Cardiff to Lisbon fell victim to a torpedo from the German submarine *U37* on December 2, 1940, resulting in the loss of seven of her crew.

And what of the legendary 'Potato' Jones who had rounded Cape Horn in sail at fourteen years of age, and brought an element of humour to that savage conflict called Spain? In the Second World War he injured his shoulder in a bombing attack on his ship, but within two months was ferrying troops from the beaches of Dunkirk. He died at home in his native Swansea in 1965 at 92 years of age.

APPENDICES

12. APPENDIX ONE

Welsh Ships Captured by Nationalist Forces

Date	*Vessel*	*Details*
4.3.1937	*Yorkbrook*	Captured by the insurgent cruiser *Canarias* with a cargo of munitions off Bilbao and was being escorted to Pasajes. Republican destroyer *Jose Luis Diez* and four armed trawlers rescued the ship and took her into Bermeo. At the time the *Yorkbrook* was flying the Estonian flag, but a measure of influence was exercised in her movements by Claude Angel of Cardiff.
14.7.1937	*Molton*	Captured by the insurgent cruiser *Almirante Cervera* while trying to enter Santander to embark refugees, and escorted to Bilbao. Released on 10.9.1937. Owners – W.J. Tatem Ltd., Cardiff, vessel registered at London. Lord Glanely was the principal shareholder in this company.
17.7.1937	*Candleston Castle*	Captured by the insurgent vessels *Velasco* and *Plus Ultra* while attempting to enter Gijon to embark refugees. Released on 10.9.1937. Owners – Branch Steamship Co. Ltd. (Reginald Jones and Co. Ltd., managers), Cardiff. Port of registry – Cardiff.
25.8.1937	*Seabank*	Seized by insurgent forces at Santander when the port was taken. Vessel was engaged in embarking refugees for France. Released on 2.9.1937. Owners – Veronica Steamship Co. Ltd., Cardiff and Porthcawl (Alfred Pope). Port of registry – Cardiff.
25.8.1937	*Kenfig Pool*	Seized by insurgent forces at Santander when the port was taken. Vessel was engaged in embarking refugees for France. Released on 2.9.1937. Owners – Kenfig Pool Export and Import Co. Ltd., Cardiff and Porthcawl (Alfred Pope). Port of registry – Gibraltar.
25.8.1937	*Seven Seas Spray*	Seized by insurgent forces at Santona when the port fell. Vessel was engaged in embarking refugees for France. Released on

Date	*Vessel*	*Details*
		1.11.1937. Owners – Veronica Steamship Co. Ltd., Cardiff and Porthcawl (Alfred Pope). Port of registry – Cardiff.
25.8.1937	*Bobie*	Seized by insurgent forces at Santona when the port fell. Vessel was engaged in embarking refugees for France. Released on 26.8.1937. Owners – W.H. McEwen, Parkston, Dorset. Port of registry – Gibraltar. On time-charter to the Veronica Steamship Co. Ltd., Cardiff and Porthcawl (Alfred Pope).
3.10.1937	*Bobie*	Captured by insurgent warship off Northern Spain whilst carrying a cargo of foodstuffs from Antwerp for either Aviles or Gijon. Ship taken to Rivadeo, but was later moved to Ferrol, arriving on 6.10.1937. Cargo confiscated and vessel released on 13.11.1937. Owners – W.H. McEwen, Parkston, Dorset. Port of registry – Gibraltar. On time-charter to the Veronica Steamship Co. Ltd., Cardiff and Porthcawl (Alfred Pope).
5.10.1937	*Yorkbrook*	Captured by insurgent warship while trying to enter Gijon to embark refugees. Released on 20.11.1937. Owners – Angel, Son and Co. Ltd., Cardiff. Port of registry – Swansea.
15.6.1938	*Isadora*	See Appendix 2 for details.
26.1.1939	*African Mariner*	See Appendix 2 for details.
26.1.1939	*Miocene*	See Appendix 2 for details.
26.1.1939	*Yorkbrook*	See Appendix 2 for details.
29.3.1939	*Dellwyn*	See Appendix 2 for details.
29.3.1939	*Lucky*	See Appendix 2 for details.

13. APPENDIX TWO
Welsh Ships Sunk by Nationalist Forces

Date	*Vessel*	*Details*
31.5.1938	*Penthames*	Bombed and sunk by insurgent aircraft while discharging a cargo of wheat and pig iron at Valenica which she had brought from Port de Bouc. No casualties. Owners – African and Continental Steamship Co. Ltd., London, (David P. Barnett, Cardiff, manager). Port of registry – London.
6.6.1938	*St. Winifred*	Bombed and badly damaged by insurgent aircraft while discharging a cargo of foodstuffs at Alicante. Five members of crew killed, and although not sunk she had to be towed to Marseilles where she was declared a Constructive Total Loss. Vessel sold in 11.1938 to Italians who following repairs placed her in service as the *Capo Vita*. Owners – The Barry Shipping Co. Ltd. (B. and S. Shipping Co. Ltd.), Cardiff. Port of registry – Newport.
9.6.1938	*Isadora*	Bombed and sunk by insurgent aircraft while discharging a cargo of wheat at Castellon which she had brought from Marseilles. No casualties. Insurgent troops took the port on 15.6.1938 and subsequently raised and repaired the vessel which was placed under the Spanish flag as the *Castillo Frias*. Owners – S. and R. Steamships Ltd., (Stone and Rolfe Ltd., managers), Llanelli and Swansea. Port of registry – Belfast.
22.6.1938	*Sunion*	Bombed and sunk by insurgent aircraft whilst lying at anchor one mile outside Valencia. She was in ballast about to take on passengers. No casualties. Owners – African and Continental Steamship Co. Ltd., London, (David P. Barnett, Cardiff, manager). Port of registry – London.
27.6.1938	*Arlon*	Bombed and set on fire by insurgent aircraft while discharging a cargo of aviation spirit at Valencia. This cargo had been brought from St. Louis, Rhone. Due to the danger the

Date	Vessel	Details
		vessel was towed out to sea, and sank off Nazaret Beach, one mile South of Valencia. One member of crew killed and another injured. Owners – Arlon Steamship Co. Ltd., London, (Jas. German and Co. Ltd., Cardiff, managers). Port of registry – London.
27.7.1938	*Dellwyn*	Bombed and sunk by insurgent aircraft while discharging a cargo of coal at Gandia. No casualties. Insurgent troops took the port on 29.3.1939 and on 10.5.1939 raised the vessel. Subsequently repaired she was placed under the Spanish flag as the *Castillo Montesa.* Owners – Dillwyn Steamship Co. Ltd., Swansea, (Angel, Son and Co. Ltd., Cardiff, managers). Port of registry – Cardiff.
23.1.1939	*African Mariner*	Bombed and sunk by insurgent aircraft while discharging at Barcelona. Four members of crew killed. Insurgent troops took the port on 26.1.1939 and on 18.4.1939 raised the vessel and following repairs placed her under the Spanish flag as the *Castillo Montjuich.* Owners – African and Continental Steamship Co. Ltd., London, (David P. Barnett, Cardiff, manager). Port of registry – London.
22.1.1939	*Yorkbrook*	Bombed and sunk by insurgent aircraft while discharging at Barcelona. No casualties. Insurgent troops took the port on 26.1.1939 and on 16.1.1940 raised the vessel and following repairs placed her under the Spanish flag as the *Castillo Monteagudo.* Owners – Angel, Son and Co. Ltd., Cardiff. Port of registry – Swansea.
24.1.1939	*Miocene*	Bombed and sunk by insurgent aircraft while discharging a cargo of benzine at Barcelona. No casualties. Insurgent troops took the port on 26.1.1939 and subsequently raised the vessel which following repairs was placed under the Spanish flag as the *Castillo Pedraza y Campanero*. Owners – Angel, Son and Co. Ltd., Cardiff. Port of registry – London.

Date	*Vessel*	*Details*
11.2.1939	*Lucky*	Bombed and sunk by insurgent aircraft while discharging at Valencia. No casualties. Insurgent troops took the port on 28.3.1939 and on 29.5.1939 raised the vessel which following repairs was placed under the Spanish flag as the *Castillo Benisano*. Owners – African and Continental Steamship Co. Ltd., London, (David P. Barnett, Cardiff, manager). Port of registry – Gibraltar.

Whilst this book has been devoted to the Welsh Blockade Runners in the Spanish Civil War, it is the author's intention to compile an expanded volume dealing with all British ships involved, including those operated by that legendary figure Jack Albert Billmeir.

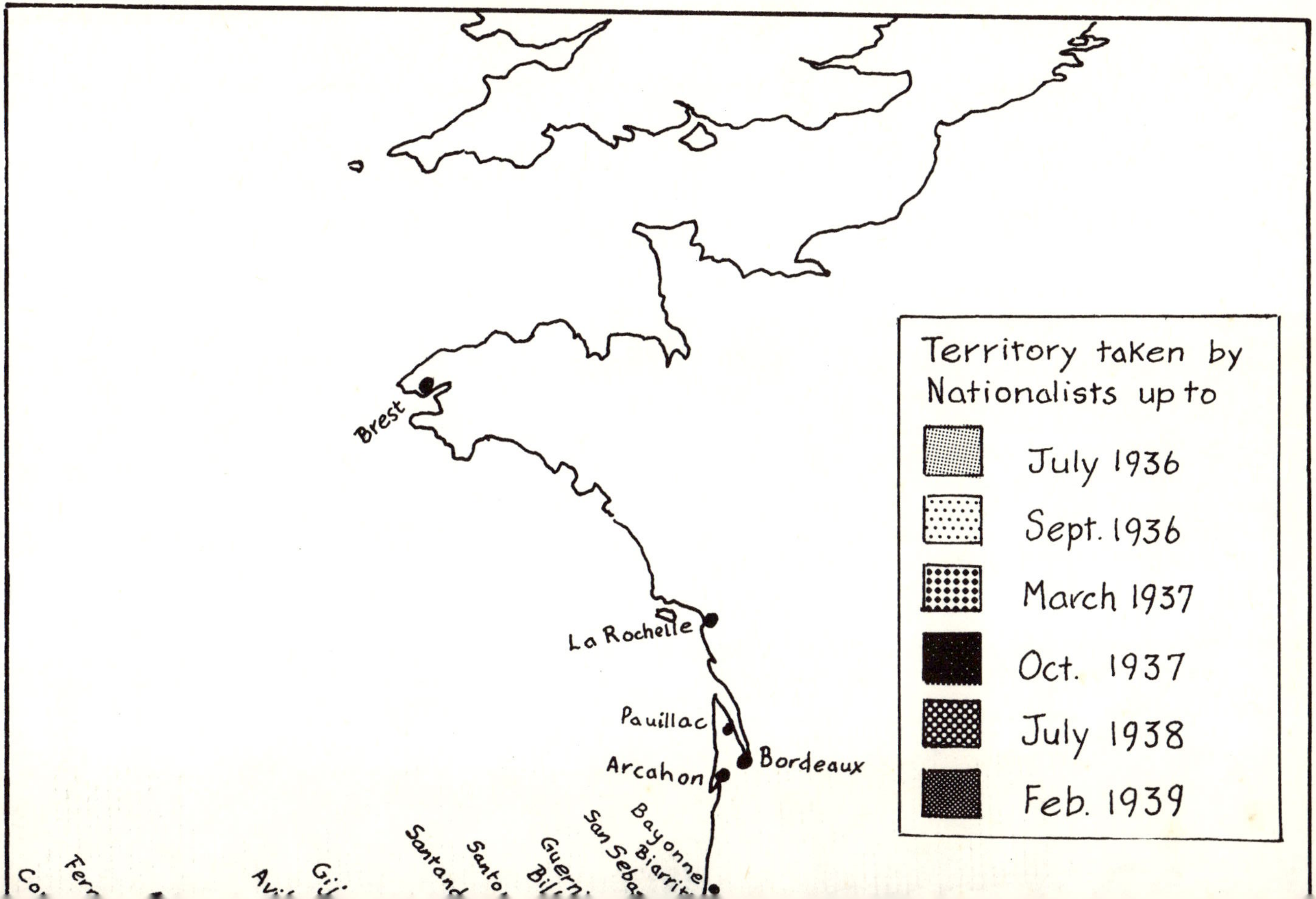
Territory taken by Nationalists up to
July 1936
Sept. 1936
March 1937
Oct. 1937
July 1938
Feb. 1939
Brest
La Rochelle
Pauillac
Bordeaux
Arcahon
Bayonne